TITHE

IS IT FOR US TODAY?

Scriptural balance to Kingdom Prosperity

DR. FELIX OKEROGHENE IDOLOR

Copyright @ 2023 by Felix Idolor

The right of Felix Idolor to be identified as the Author of this Work has been asserted by him in accordance with the Copyright, Designs and Patents Act 1988.

Self-published in South Africa in 2023.

All rights reserved. No part if this publication may be reproduced, stored in a retrieval system, or transmitted, in any form or by any means without the prior written permission of the publisher, nor be otherwise circulated and without a similar condition being imposed on the subsequent purchaser.

The Holy Bible used in this book is New King James Version
Copyright © 1982 by Thomas Nelson, Inc.

ISBN 979-8877985971

Project coordinator: Red Mouse Design and Publication

Printed and bound by Bidvest Data

"BEHOLD, THIS WE HAVE
SEARCHED OUT;
IT IS TRUE.
HEAR IT, AND KNOW
FOR YOURSELF."

JOB 5:27

Contents

Chapter 1: FIRST WORDS 7

Chapter 2: RETURN TO ME 15

Chapter 3: THE ANSWER TO POVERTY 19

Chapter 4: THE JUBILEE IS HERE.. 23

Chapter 5: FINANCIAL PEACE.. 27

Chapter 6: GOD'S FINANCIAL PLAN 30

Chapter 7: COVENANT OF PROSPERITY............................... 35

Chapter 8: PRESCRIPTION FOR FINANCIAL
PROSPERITY.. 40

Chapter 9: GET BACK ON PLAN.. 44

Chapter 10: TITHING AND YOUR FINANCES 50

Chapter 11: PRINCIPLES AND PRACTICE 55

Chapter 12: THE RULE OF FIRST MENTION 61

Chapter 13: TRANSITION TO A NEW PRIESTHOOD 68

Chapter 14: THE TITHE: LAW OR GRACE? 74

Chapter 15: JESUS CHRIST, MELCHIZEDEK
AND THE TITHE 79

Chapter 16: THE STATEMENTS OF JESUS CHRIST
ABOUT THE TITHE 83

Chapter 17: GOD'S FINANCIAL PLAN FOR THE GOSPEL.... 94

Chapter 18: BLESSING PARTNERSHIP OF TITHING 99

Chapter 19: AM I CURSED FOR NOT TITHING?................... 102

Chapter 20: GRACE REMOVES THE PRESSURE 107

Chapter 21: LOVE'S APPEAL FOR PARTNERSHIP 114

Chapter 22: THE HELPING HANDS OF TITHERS 117

Chapter 23: TITHE AND WEALTH CREATION 123

Chapter 24: STEPS TO SUCCESSFUL TITHING 129

Chapter 25: THE GREATEST USE OF MONEY 148

RECEIVE JESUS CHRIST AS LORD 154

WELCOME TO THE FAMILY OF GOD! 157

OTHER BOOKS BY DR. FELIX O. IDOLOR 158

REFERENCES 159

1

FIRST WORDS

Malachi 1:1:
"The burden of the word of the Lord to Israel by Malachi."

The temple in Jerusalem had been rebuilt following the decree of Cyrus, the king, that Jews could return to their land, rebuild their temple and freely worship their God. The wall of Jerusalem had also been rebuilt and the coming of Israel's messiah was on the horizon.

The spiritual condition of the people was however on the decline again. Their spiritual leaders, the priests, were lacklustre in their worship, not having the honour and fear of God at heart, they placed their own interests above the interest of God and the people. The poor were oppressed and a general disdain for religion caused a decline in support for the temple and this was all reflected in a general economic decline.

God was not through with Israel despite the situation. His providential care had seen them through the captivity and brought them back to the land. However, to turn things around God would have to send them His word because true to His character He does nothing without his word.

Amos 3:7:
"Surely the Lord God does nothing,
Unless He reveals His secret to His servants the prophets."

God had to send His word through the prophet Malachi to the people. The prophet Malachi introduced His prophetic message with the words:

"The burden of the word of the Lord to Israel by Malachi."

The prophet refers to his message as a burden. Jesus Christ said, "My yoke is easy, and my burden is light" (Matt 11:30). Malachi's message is not a burden that brings grief and creates bondage. The word of God comes to set us free. There is however a burden of responsibility that comes with the word of God. James instructs us to be doers of God's word and not hearers only (James 1:22).

The Hebrew word for burden is "masa" and it means a load, that which is to be lifted and carried and to labour. Then it means "that to which the soul lifts itself". In other words, your aspiration.

The word of the Lord comes to us where we are no matter how messy our circumstances are or how messed up our lives are, but it never leaves us there. The word comes to transform our lives.

God's word calls on us to lift our souls or our minds from the mundane to something higher, a higher calling. That is precisely what the prophet's message to the people was sent to achieve. The word of the Lord came to lift the people from the morass of spiritual decline to the higher ground of being co-workers with God in ushering the advent of the Messiah. Their finances were not left out of that calling.

When we are preoccupied with the mundane, we fail to see the link between the spiritual, higher things of heaven and our tedious financial matters.

God's people in the time of Malachi had also stopped seeing the connection between the two. The prophetic word came to correct this notion in their minds and make them see how disobedience in financial matters can spiral into every area of life and leave us overwhelmed where we do not even know where to start picking up the pieces.

Many times, when the subject of finances is broached people automatically think of it in selfish terms as if it were all about pleasing ourselves in this world. We erroneously think it is all about having food to eat, dressing in fashionable clothing, driving the best cars, and living in palatial homes. But the Bible says God has pleasure in the prosperity of His servants (Psalm 35:27). Real Bible prosperity has an eternal value to it and never leaves you where you are. God builds your character, prepares you for eternity and makes you a blessing to your fellow human beings in this world and at the same time works in you and through you to meet your financial needs.

Malachi called the Lord's message to the people a burden. He had to live by his own message but then he also had to give it to the people and once the message was given to them, it became their own load to carry. In other words, they had a responsibility from God to follow through on the instructions therein.

Responsibility is the hallmark of maturity. Malachi's message therefore is a call to maturity. There can be no real maturity that does not touch our finances. God calls on us to see ourselves as His stewards in financial matters and to handle our financial matters with kingdom diligence and responsibility. This is a lofty ideal to which we should all aspire and stretch ourselves. The word of God has been sent to get us there if we are willing and obedient.

Galatians 6:5:

"For each one shall bear his own load."

The Apostle refers here to the Roman soldier's survival kit. Every one of those soldiers had to carry his own survival kit as they marched into battle.

It was estimated that an average Roman soldier could carry up to 50 kilograms in the form of his survival kit which was divided between his armour, his weapons, and personal luggage. The Roman's soldier survival kit included spare clothing, food rations, basic cooking utensils, first aid items and personal hygiene items. It was suicidal as a soldier not to carry your survival kit. No one could carry your survival kit for you. You had to do it yourself.

Malachi's reference to His message as a burden, a load, fits right into Paul's metaphor of the Roman's soldier's survival kit.

The word of God, contained in the Bible, is all that we need to survive the challenging times we live in. It is our responsibility, however, to study and meditate on it for ourselves and become doers of it.

The English word "survive" means to outlive. God wants us to outlive and outlast whatever circumstances the enemy brings to cut short God's plans for our lives. To survive also means to live above. God wants to bring to us the power to rise above the circumstances of life and stay on top and God has not left out the area of our finances from this.

If the Israelites were to survive the challenges of their time, which included difficult financial circumstances, they needed to take Malachi's prophetic message to heart and become doers of it. To them it was the equivalent of the Roman soldier's survival kit.

Today we are witnessing the rapid spiral of events toward the soon return of the Lord Jesus Christ. Time and prophetic events are being compressed like never before. Advanced information technology enables us to see daily the fulfilment of end-time Bible prophecy.

The urgency to prepare ourselves for the soon return of our King, the Lord Jesus Christ, has never been greater.

Just as in the times of Malachi the prophet, we face political and economic upheavals like never before and the challenge of living godly lives amid a general spiritual and religious apathy has never been steeper.

God in His goodness came through to the people with a message which was their survival kit: The burden of the word of the Lord through His prophet Malachi.

Like the Roman soldier, every one of them was responsible for picking it up and utilising the instructions therein to survive the times in which they lived. That message is still valid for today.

Isaiah 40:8:
**"The grass withers, the flower fades,
But the word of our God stands forever."**

The subject of finances when mentioned in church stirs up controversy today as it has always done.

There are those who think that spirituality, godliness, and finances do not mix just as oil and water cannot mix.

Then there those who assume that every time a preacher talks about money, he is about to religiously manipulate people to give up their hard-earned cash. In this regard debate and controversy about the tithe and tithing rages in Christian circles and in the world. Where exactly lies the truth?

If we approach God's word with prayerful, honest, and open hearts, we can find the truth with the help of the Holy Spirit. Jesus Christ the head of the church said that much.

John 16:13:

"However, when He, the Spirit of truth, has come, He will guide you into all truth; for He will not speak on His own authority, but whatever He hears He will speak; and He will tell you things to come."

To be teachable by the Holy Spirit we must come to God's word and be willing to lay aside our biases and preconceived notions.

Job 5:27:

"Behold, this we have searched out;
It is true. Hear it, and know for yourself."

This is the key to building our lives on a solid foundation that will last for all times.

We need to search the word of God and dig into it until we know it for ourselves. We take personal possession of it. It becomes our personal truth. You get to the place where it is as though the Bible were God physically standing there talking to you and addressing you, your life and circumstances.

When we apply this principle in the financial area then it does not matter what people's opinions are. We can live our lives based on the eternal truth of God's word.

The Hebrew word translated as "search" in Job 5.27 is an intensive word. It denotes intensive activity. It implies the application of all of one's effort. It means to dig for essence and to investigate.

It is like the crime detective following the trail of evidence from a crime scene with an unbiased mind. All he is interested in is the truth and he is willing to follow the trail of evidence until he comes to the verdict of the truth which allows him to apprehend the culprit.

The word "search" means "bringing up from the depth". This is how to approach the word of God. You don't come with preconceived notions and ideas, but you allow the word of God to correct your preconceived notions and ideas.

You certainly don't come to the word of God to twist it and bend it to make it say what you want it to say. You allow the word of God to lead you to the truth.

This is my approach in this study about the tithe and I urge you to let this be your attitude as well.

Job 5:27 says: "… we have searched these things out and found it to be so". The Hebrew word translated as "so" is the word "ken" and it means "that which is fixed and established and will never change".

Psalm 119:89:

"Forever, O Lord,

Your word is settled in heaven."

Jesus said those who came to Him and heard His words and put His words into practice were like the wise builder who dug deep and laid his foundation on the rock. That rock is fixed permanently in place and will never move or change.

The doers of His word did not just hear it, they took the time to dig into it until they found out from the word of God that it was the established truth, an eternal law and principle of God that will never change. Then they based their entire life and existence on it, and it upheld, sustained, and carried them through the storms of life. When the storms of life came after them, they would not change. They continued consistently in it, knowing that "these things are so".

If we do not have truth as the foundation of our lives when the storms of life come, we crumble.

This is the same attitude that the Berean Christians had.

Acts 17:11-12:

"These were more fair-minded than those in Thessalonica, in that they received the word with all readiness, and searched the Scriptures daily to find out whether these things were so. Therefore many of them believed, and also not a few of the Greeks, prominent women as well as men."

The Bible refers to them as fair-minded. The Greek word used here also means "good" or "excellent breed". They were an excellent breed of Christians. People who had in them the quality to rise to the top.

They went to God's word for themselves and searched it until they found that the things the apostle Paul was teaching were the eternal truths of God's word and then they based their faith on it. When the storms of life came to them, they would remain consistent in their faith.

This book is a study about the tithe and tithing. My aim is to follow the trail of evidence from the Old Testament into the New Testament and let the word of God bring out the eternal truth of God on which we can base our convictions.

Much more than the tithe however, it is study about God's love revealed in the Person of Jesus Christ and His intensive desire to be involved in every area of our lives including our finances. God has stretched out His helping hands to us in all areas of our lives in the person of Jesus Christ. It is up to us to take hold of it through His word.

Financial matters tend to be controversial, stirring up intensive interests with all kinds of emotions, and that rightfully so because from a natural prospect money is a scarce resource.

To be called upon to release ten percent of your hard and honestly earned money amid urgent and pressing financial concerns should certainly raise your eyebrows.

The burden of responsibility is therefore on individuals to do their due diligence and know the truth for themselves when it comes to tithing.

Malachi's reference to his prophetic message as "the burden of the word of the Lord" is therefore a fitting title in this regard. It is a call on our part to a diligent study which leads to knowledge of the truth.

I urge you to study this book prayerfully with an open mind taking the time to look up the Scriptures referenced in it.

Some Scriptural quotations have been repeated several times as is the nature of a Bible study but each time there is a Scripture repetition, please pay attention to catch onto the point that is being highlighted.

As you embark on this study, I pray that the Apostle John's three-dimensional prayer be realised in your life.

"Beloved, I pray that you may prosper in all things and be in health, just as your soul prospers" (3 John:2).

2

RETURN TO ME

> Malachi 3:6:
> "For I am the Lord, I do not change;
> Therefore you are not consumed, O sons of Jacob.
> Yet from the days of your fathers You have gone away from
> My ordinances
> And have not kept them.
> Return to Me, and I will return to you,"
> Says the Lord of hosts.
> "But you said,
> 'In what way shall we return?'"

The prophetic word comes to Israel as the dark spiritual decline and economic turmoil loomed over the nation. The God of Abraham, Isaac and Jacob had not forsaken them and if they would return to Him, He would turn their circumstances around and take them to future glory.

The question that naturally came to their minds was: "Where do we start to return from?"

God, through the prophet Malachi, gave them the key to the change they needed and where they could begin to see a supernatural turnaround of their circumstances.

In Malachi 3 He said to them: "Return to Me, and I will return to you."

Life can be so overwhelming and circumstances so perplexing that we seem to lose our bearings in life. We hardly know where we are, how we got where we are and how to proceed.

God, however, is never at a loss about us and our circumstances. He always knows where we are and how to deliver us.

The Hebrew word for return is "shoab" and it means to return to the starting point. It means to return to a former state or condition. Then God identifies the starting or point of origin to them. He said to them: "Yet from the days of your fathers you have departed from My ordinances." If their circumstances would be turned around supernaturally God identifies where it would all begin.

Proverbs 22:28:
"Do not remove the ancient landmark
Which your fathers have set."

When it comes to the subject of prosperity there are laws and principles that transcend time and generations, and we ignore them at our own perils. This is what the children of Israel had done at the time prophet Malachi spoke to them. They had departed from principles of financial success by which God dealt with their fathers and the prophet Malachi calls their attention to these principles of God.

The apostle Paul writing in the New Testament respected ancient landmarks. He recognised that there are certain timeless principles by which God dealt with people whether under the old or New Testament.

2 Timothy 1:3:
"I thank God, whom I serve with a pure conscience, as my forefathers did, as without ceasing I remember you in my prayers night and day."

Paul living in the new covenant honoured the timeless principles of service and worship that God laid down for us through the forefathers.

When God cut the covenant with the fathers, Abraham, Isaac and Jacob, one of the first areas He dealt with was their finances. He taught them to trust Him with their lives especially in their finances because He knew if that was not taken care of it would eventually affect every other area of their lives. He gave them financial laws that would ensure that they looked to Him and Him alone for their finances and that money and material things would never be their gods.

Look at Abraham! What was the first thing God dealt with him when he departed from Ur of the Chaldees? It was his finances. Abraham made a commitment to God never to look to man for finances but to trust God completely and totally as his source to get his needs met. There Abraham left an ancient landmark for generations to come.

It was the starting point. That was the basis upon which their fathers lived in financial prosperity in covenant relationship with God.

What was the final straw that brought divine judgement upon Israel and the eventual carrying away of the nation into captivity? It was their refusal to continue with God's instructions concerning having their material needs being met. They began to imitate the practices of the godless nations that surrounded them. Israel took to the fertility cults of Baal and Asherah in the false hope that these gods would bring prosperity to them.

Not following God's instructions in financial matters can have serious ramifications on all areas of our lives.

Now through the prophet Malachi God calls upon them to get back to the beginning point.

He calls them to get back to where He started off dealing with them which was in trusting Him in their finances.

If you can't trust God in your finances, you won't be able to trust God with other areas of your life.

Through the prophet Malachi, God said to them: "But you said, 'In what shall we return?'" (Mal 3:7).

"What" is an interrogative word which in the Hebrew can mean "what", "where", "when", "how much".

In other words, the questions that naturally came to their minds as He spoke to them were: "What is this starting point, where is this starting point, when is it and how much is it?"

This is when God brings up the subject of tithing.

In this study we shall delve into the Bible to find the answers for these questions in relation to tithe and tithing.

God began His dealings with the covenant fathers in this area of finances because He wanted no limits to what His power could do in their lives. God has not changed. This is His attitude toward us today.

God wants us to cooperate with Him so He can move unhindered in every area of our lives.

Our refusal to trust God in our finances will stop the flow of God's power into other areas of our lives.

The mighty move of God in the end times that has been much prophesied about will not happen until God's people learn to trust Him fully with their finances.

Those who are going to walk with God and work with Him to bring about the greatest outpouring of His power in the history of mankind are those who will obey God in their finances. It will be those who have learned to trust God fully with their finances.

3

THE ANSWER TO POVERTY

Luke 4:18-19:
"The Spirit of the Lord is upon Me,
Because He has anointed Me
To preach the gospel to the poor;
He has sent Me to heal the brokenhearted,
To proclaim liberty to the captives
And recovery of sight to the blind,
To set at liberty those who are oppressed;
To proclaim the acceptable year of the Lord."

One of the biggest problems people have to contend with today is the problem of a lack of money. The vast majority of people struggle daily to have their needs met and in the African continent poverty is one of the biggest problems.

The failure of governments throught their various policies and programmes to address this issue of poverty is very glaring and the reason is obvious. A look at the problem of poverty through the lens of Scriptures will show us that poverty is first and foremost a spiritual problem before it is a physical problem showing up in man's inability to meet his needs.

There is a place for government and its policies in creating an environment where people can take charge of their lives and thrive, but government per se is not the answer for poverty. Jesus gave us the answer to poverty in the above verses: "The Spirit of the Lord is upon Me, Because He has anointed Me to preach the gospel to the poor."

The Greek word translated as "preach" here is "kerruso" and this word was associated with kings and their kingdoms in the those days.

The "kerruso" was the one who went to the city center or village sqaure at a sutiable time when all could hear and made announcements to the people from the king. He was the king's spokesman and whatever he announced, was the official information from the government of the day revealing the government's position on a matter. He annnounced the policies and programmes of the king to the people.

Jesus said: "The spirit of the Lord is upon Me to preach or announce the gospel as the kingdom's official position and attitude and answer toward the subject of poverty."

In other words, Jesus' message was a public declaration of heaven's official position and policy toward the earth and its inhabitants. In the message we see God's attitude toward the problems that bedevil us here on earth, which includes poverty.

IS POVERTY THE WILL OF GOD ?

By following Jesus and His message we can see God's attitude toward poverty. Is poverty God's will? Well, we can know by just listening to Jesus's message and His actions. Remember He said: "The Spirit of the Lord is upon Me, for He has anointed Me to preach the gospel." In other words, to announce and demonstrate it so that all human beings can know heaven's position and attitude toward poverty."

The gospel of Jesus Chrsit reveals that God is not only against poverty but has provided the comprehensive answer for it and that answer is available for everybody everywhere.

God's answer for poverty is the gospel of Jesus Christ.

AS IN HEAVEN SO ON EARTH

Matthew 6:9-13:
"In this manner, therefore, pray:
Our Father in heaven,
Hallowed be Your name.
Your kingdom come.

> Your will be done
> On earth as it is in heaven.
> Give us this day our daily bread.
> And forgive us our debts,
> As we forgive our debtors.
> And do not lead us into temptation,
> But deliver us from the evil one.
> For Yours is the kingdom and the power and the glory."

Jesus taught His disciples how to pray in these verses. First He called God Father and the very idea of Father excludes poverty from His nature. We all derive our fatherhood nature from God and there is no father that wants to see his children go through life miserable with their needs unmet. Every father's dream and desire is to see that their children's need are adequately taken care of and that is God's desire for every person.

Then Jesus goes on to teach us to pray: "'Your will be done on earth, as it is in heaven."

We simply need to ask ourselves the question: "are there people in heaven wallowing in the misery of poverty going around with their needs unmet?" None whatsoever. That must be God's will for everybody on earth then. It is God's will that you and I and every one else have our needs adequately met. He has made the provision for this and all we need to do is learn how to tap into His provisions from the word of God.

2 Peter 1:2-3:

> "Grace and peace be multiplied to you in the knowledge of God and of Jesus our Lord, as His divine power has given to us all things that pertain to life and godliness, through the knowledge of Him who called us by glory and virtue."

Notice Scripture says "His divine power has given to us all things that pertain to life and godliness ..." That means the provision has been made. It says His provision covers all things pertaining to life and godliness. Do finances pertain to life? Certainly it does, because no one can get around this world without finances. What about godliness? Do finances have anything to do with godliness? Yes! We can certainly use money to promote godliness in this world by using money to promote the gospel which causes people to live a godly life in this world. This means God has made His power available to cause our financial needs to be met while we live in this world. The power can be there however without it working for you just like you can have electricity cables carrying power through the the city where you live and still be living in darkness without the benefit of electricity. You have to get connected to the power and then operate according to the laws that govern electricity to have that power working for your benefit.

For God's power to work to cause our financial needs to be met we must learn to operate according to the laws that govern His power.

Deuteronomy 8:18:

"And you shall remember the Lord your God, for it is He who gives you power to get wealth, that He may establish His covenant which He swore to your fathers, as it is this day."

The power has been made available but we have to put it to work for us on earth. That is our part as human beings and that is where people fail and the reason for this failure is lack of knowledge. It is ignorance of God's provisions that holds people in the bondage of poverty today and not because it is the will of God.

Hosea 4:6:
"My people are destroyed for lack of knowledge.
Because you have rejected knowledge,
I also will reject you from being priest for Me;
Because you have forgotten the law of your God,
I also will forget your children."

People are perishing in poverty today not because it is the will of God for them but because of a lack of knowledge of God's provisions.

4

THE JUBILEE IS HERE

Let's look at Luke 4:18-21 again but reading this time from the Passion translation.

"The spirit of the Lord is upon me, and he has anointed me to be hope for the poor, freedom for the broken hearted, and new eyes for the blind, and to preach to prisoners, 'you are set free' I have come to share the message of jubilee, 'for the time of God's great acceptance' has begun".

Jesus is quoting Isaiah 61:1-2 which are verses about the jubilee, and He began to teach them how it could come into effect in their lives. He taught them saying: " This Scripture is fulfilled in your hearing."

Remember the word "preach" is a declaration of an official policy of the king or government to the people. Jesus Christ was declaring to the people God's official policy toward them and that was the "jubilee".

The jubilee was proclaimed in Israel every 50 years, and it was a year of supernatural debt cancellation where all the poor and landless returned to possession of land and property and had the opportunity once again to build a life of prosperity and live debt free.

The jubilee went into effect on the day of atonement.

"The day of atonement and the jubilee had much in common. The message of both was the new birth. The day of atonement freed man from the slavery to sin and enabled him to start a new life, at one with God and his fellow man. The jubilee had for its aim the emancipation of the individual from the shackles of poverty and the readjustment of various strata in the commonwealth in accordance with social justice. No more appropriate day therefore for inaugurating such a year of rectification" (The Pentateuch and the Haftorah,1960).

"With the blast of the jubilee trumpet the slave goes free, and a redivision of the lands secures again to the poorest his fair share in the of bounty the common Creator" (Henry George, quoted in the Pentateuch and Haftorah).

In other words, with the proclamation of the jubilee every Israelite had equal access to God's great bounty. This is the gospel which Jesus Christ preached and taught. This is how He explained God's attitude toward the poor and downtrodden.

God created this earth and decked it with wealth more than enough for everyone. He never planned for some to be stupendously rich and have more than enough for their needs while others had little or nothing to get by. This inequality has been addressed through the sacrifice of Jesus on the cross and the knowledge of this is to be brought to all people through the preaching and teaching of the gospel.

Without this knowledge multitudes in our world will continue to wallow in poverty and misery despite the price that Jesus paid on the cross to deliver us from it.

The gospel levels the playing field and gives all people on earth equal access to the wealth of this world to have their needs met through the power of God. This is what the jubilee is about.

The jubilee meant supernatural debt cancellation and if you are in debt and do not know how you will get out of it, the gospel of Jesus Christ is a proclamation of jubilee which makes you realise that God wants you out of debt and offers you His supernatural power to get you out of it.

Luke 4:20-21:
"Then He closed the book, and gave it back to the attendant and sat down. And the eyes of all who were in the synagogue were fixed on Him. And He began to say to them, 'Today this Scripture is fulfilled in your hearing.'"

He began to teach them from these verses in Isaiah 61:1-2:

He explained to them how these Scriptures would work to produce the desired outcome in their lives. In the same way it would work today in our lives.

Jesus explained to them that "this Scripture is fulfilled in your hearing". That was the main point or summary of all He was teaching or explaining to them. In other words, the jubilee or God's supernatural prosperity would not happen just because it was provided and available to them. They had something to do with entering the benefits of it. They had to hear it for it to be fulfilled. The jubilee would come into effect, and they could access supernatural debt cancellation and equal access to the earth's wealth by hearing it.

Jesus was not talking about hearing His message with their physical ears because they had just heard Him teaching it and yet wanted to throw Him off the cliff. He was speaking about hearing it with their inner ears: the ears of their heart or spirits. In other words, getting a revelation and an understanding of it in their hearts.

What does the Bible say about hearing God's word?

Romans 10:17:
"So then faith comes by hearing,
and hearing by the word of God."
The jubilee was available to them, but it could only be fulfilled
by faith that comes from hearing the word of God.

Without faith no one can enter the provisions of God, and we cannot have faith beyond our knowledge of God's word. If you don't know the provision is available you can't have faith for it, and you can't access it. You are cut off from it.

This what Hosea 4:6 explains:

"My people are destroyed for lack of knowledge.
Because you have rejected knowledge,
I also will reject you from being priest for Me;
Because you have forgotten the law of your God,
I also will forget your children."

The Hebrew word "destroyed" also means "to cut off.' Ignorance cuts people off the provisions of God.

The jubilee is available now through the once for all time sacrifice of Jesus Christ at the cross, but because of ignorance people are cut off from it. One major reason for that is religion which tries to sanctify and glorify poverty as if God had any pleasure in it and wants people poor to keep them humble. Poverty does not make anybody humble. It only creates an appearance of false humility.

5

FINANCIAL PEACE

Luke 4:21 tells us that Jesus Christ began to say: "This day this Scripture is fulfilled in your hearing. "

In the Aramaic translation the word "Shalem" is translated as "fulfil". This is the word "shalom" which is translated from the Hebrew Bible as "peace" in the English.

His message was a message of peace, and the subject of our finances is part of that peace.

Peter, under the inspiration of the Holy Spirit, summarized the message and ministry of Jesus Christ to us in Acts 10:36-38:

"The word which God sent to the children of Israel, preaching peace through Jesus Christ – He is Lord of all – that word you know, which was proclaimed throughout all Judea, and began from Galilee after the baptism which John preached: how God anointed Jesus of Nazareth with the Holy Spirit and with power, who went about doing good and healing all who were oppressed by the devil, for God was with Him."

His entire message was a message of peace, and we can see now that our finances are included in that peace. The gospel of Jesus Christ is a gospel of peace and that includes financial peace. Every time you see the word "peace" in Scriptures, you should see your finances included in it. After all, one of the greatest areas of worry, anxiety, and fear to people in this world is finances. Worrying about finances and how our needs will be met is one area of temptation that the devil uses to steal the word of God out of the hearts of people.

Matthew 13:22:

"Now he who received seed among the thorns is he who hears the word, and the cares of this world and the deceitfulness of riches choke the word, and he becomes unfruitful."

This word "cares" means "worries and anxiety". It means that which splits and divides the mind. These people did not know how to operate in the financial peace of God and so the devil stole the word of God from their hearts.

Notice that Jesus did not say money or riches choked the word of God from their hearts. He said: "deceitfulness of riches" did that. In other words, they lacked the knowledge of Bible truth about finances and the devil exploited their ignorance to deceive them about money and stole the word of God from them. You could be living in poverty and be deceived about finances and ignorance will allow the devil to keep stealing God's word from your heart and thereby keep you in poverty with your needs unmet. One way the devil does this very well is by dressing poverty, lack and want with religious clothes making it look as if it is the will of God and an instrument by which God keeps His saints humble. Nothing could be further from the truth, and this religious deception is part of "the deceitfulness of riches".

Let us notice Luke 4.21 in the Passion translation says: "I have come to share the message of Jubilee, for the time of God's great acceptance has begun."

The proclamation of the financial jubilee is therefore included in the Hebrew conception of peace or shalom. The word Hebrew 'Shalom' means to bring to completion or fulfilment. It signifies the fulfilment of an oath or completion of an undertaking. The word also implies 'to make good', 'to restore' and 'to make financial payment'.

Jesus was teaching about bringing the jubilee into fulfilment or completion in the lives of people. This is financial peace. Notice that the word 'shalom' also means 'to make financial payment'.

What do you pay with when you go shopping? You know the answer to that. You pay with money. So, this is also addressing your finances. That means having the financial resources to pay for your needs. Jesus came so we can have financial peace, which means having the financial resources to pay for our material needs in this world.

God wants you to have financial peace and be free from the worry and anxiety that comes with the uncertainty of not knowing from where your needs will be met. He wants you to look to Him as your source of total supply and He has a plan to bring full supply into your life. We only need to gain the knowledge of His financial plan from His word and learn to diligently follow His plan as laid out in the Scriptures.

6

GOD'S FINANCIAL PLAN

Jeremiah 29:11: (in the Classic Amplified Translation)
"For I know the thoughts and plans that I have for you, says the Lord, thoughts and plans for welfare and peace and not for evil, to give you hope in your final outcome."

God says He has a plan for our welfare and peace. We have seen that the jubilee of debt freedom and financial peace is included in this peace.

We can therefore imply that God has a financial plan for His people and if His people follow His plan, they can enjoy His supernatural financial supply.

The Lord Jesus Christ taught the people by saying to them: "This day is this Scripture fulfilled in your hearing." He was speaking about activating God's power and provisions for our lives by faith because faith comes by hearing and hearing by the word of God (Rom 10:17).

It is by faith we gain access to God's provisions of grace.

Romans 5:1-2
"Therefore, having been justified by faith, we have peace with God through our Lord Jesus Christ, through whom also we have access by faith into this grace in which we stand, and rejoice in hope of the glory of God."

It says, "having been justified by faith, we have peace with God through Jesus Christ". That includes our jubilee of freedom from debt and the peace of having the financial resources to pay for our material needs in this world. Every time you see the word "peace" in the Scriptures make it your duty to include your finances in it. In doing so you will renew your thinking to see your needs being met in Christ Jesus.

Notice it says: " It is by faith we enter this grace." Which grace is this? It is speaking about the grace of justification and peace.

What does it mean "to be justified"? It means "to be declared righteous". To be declared free from sin, guilt and condemnation. That is based on the sacrifice of Jesus Christ for us all at the cross.

2 Corinthians 5:21:
"For He made Him who knew no sin to be sin for us, that we might become the righteousness of God in Him."

The cross was the place of exchange. That is where Jesus Christ exchanged our sin, our guilt, condemnation and judgment and punishment for His own righteousness and peace with God.

When we accept what He did for us at the cross and confess His Lordship we are declared righteous, and we can have peace with God.

Romans 10:6-10:
"But the righteousness of faith speaks in this way, 'Do not say in your heart, Who will ascend into heaven?' (that is, to bring Christ down from above) or, 'Who will descend into the abyss?' (that is, to bring Christ up from the dead). But what does it say? 'The word is near you, in your mouth and in your heart' (that is, the word of faith which we preach): 'that if you confess with your mouth the Lord Jesus and believe in your heart that God has raised Him from the dead, you will be saved. For with the heart one believes unto righteousness, and with the mouth confession is made unto salvation.'"

The Holy Spirit through the apostle Paul gives us insight into how God's plan works to bring about salvation in every area of life here. It is a plan based on faith. We have to believe it with our hearts and confess with our mouths.

You are not going to enjoy God's financial peace if all you do is talk about how your needs are not being met and your bills are piling up and you are about to drown in debt!

Learn to line your words with what God has declared about you in His word. Begin to declare Jesus Christ as your financial jubilee and confess God as your source and God will make His word good in your life. Confess in the face of lack and want: "My God shall supply all your need according to His riches in glory by Christ Jesus" (Philippians 4:19).

Learn to confess Psalm 23 in the face of lack, want and difficult circumstances: "The Lord is my shepherd; I shall not want.... He prepares a table before me in the presence of my enemies... He anoints my head with oil... my cup runs over."

Read through Scriptures diligently asking God through His Holy Spirit to enlighten you to His financial plan for your life and as you get insight into this plan, become a doer of God's word because it is the doer of the word of God that is blessed.

Psalm 119:105:
"Your word is a lamp to my feet
And a light to my path."

God will guide you into financial peace through His word but learn to do the word of God because disobedience will always turn off the light in your spirit. Make a commitment to God that as He reveals His financial plan to you through His written word you will be a doer of the word and not a hearer only.

James 1:22:25:
"But be doers of the word, and not hearers only, deceiving yourselves. For if anyone is a hearer of the word and not a doer, he is like a man observing his natural face in a mirror; for he observes himself, goes away, and immediately forgets what kind of man he was. But he who looks into the perfect law of liberty and continues in it, and is not a forgetful hearer

> **but a doer of the work,**
> **this one will be blessed in what he does."**

James says, "It is the doer of the word that is blessed". To be blessed includes having your financial needs met. When we put God's financial plan into operation by acting on His word, we get the desired outcome of having financial peace in our lives which includes having our financial needs met and our bills paid.

FOUNDATION OF GOD'S WORD

God takes no pleasure in seeing anybody in poverty and living in financial distress of debts and unpaid bills.

> **Psalm 35:27:**
> **"Let them shout for joy and be glad,**
> **Who favor my righteous cause;**
> **And let them say continually,**
> **'Let the Lord be magnified,**
> **Who has pleasure in the prosperity of His servant.'"**

There is no need for God's people to be in the dark in any area of life because the Father through Jesus has sent the Holy Spirit to guide us into all truth.

> **John 16:13:**
> **"However, when He, the Spirit of truth, has come, He will guide you into all truth; for He will not speak on His own authority, but whatever He hears He will speak; and He will tell you things to come."**

The Holy Spirit will guide us into the truth using the Scriptures. We must however not give our private interpretation to Scripture.

2 Peter 1:19-21:

"And so we have the prophetic word confirmed, which you do well to heed as a light that shines in a dark place, until the day dawns and the morning star rises in your hearts; knowing this first, that no prophecy of Scripture is of any private interpretation, for prophecy never came by the will of man, but holy men of God spoke as they were moved by the Holy Spirit."

It says no prophecy of Scripture is of any private interpretation. We have no right to attach our own interpretation to the word of God, but we must allow the Holy Spirit to interpret Scripture to us with Scripture.

7

COVENANT OF PROSPERITY

Let's begin our investigation of the place of the tithe in God's financial plan from what is perhaps the most popular and contentious Scripture on the subject.

Malachi 3:6-12:
"'For I am the Lord, I do not change;
Therefore you are not consumed, O sons of Jacob.
Yet from the days of your fathers
You have gone away from My ordinances
And have not kept them.
Return to Me, and I will return to you,'
Says the Lord of hosts.
'But you said, "In what way shall we return?"'
'Will a man rob God?
Yet you have robbed Me!
But you say,
"In what way have we robbed You?"
'In tithes and offerings.
You are cursed with a curse,
For you have robbed Me,
Even this whole nation.
Bring all the tithes into the storehouse,
That there may be food in My house,
And try Me now in this,'
Says the Lord of hosts,
'If I will not open for you the windows of heaven
And pour out for you such blessing.
That there will not be
room enough to receive it.

> 'And I will rebuke the devourer for your sakes,
> So that he will not destroy the fruit of your ground,
> Nor shall the vine fail to bear fruit for you in the field,'
> Says the Lord of hosts;
> 'And all nations will call you blessed,
> For you will be a delightful land,'
> Says the Lord of hosts."

God begins by telling the people: "I am the Lord, I change not" The Hebrew word LORD is God's covenant name. It is spelt "yod-hey-vav-hey" in Hebrew.

It is generally believed that the pronunciation of this word is not known today. It is a name that carries so much reverence among the Israelites that they generally do not pronounce it but refer to it as "Hashem" which means "The Name" or "Adonai" which signifies "most high" or "Lord". Other translators use the word "Jehovah" in translating this name of God. However, the word is associated with the covenant, and it always refers to God in exercise of His lovingkindness towards His covenant people. What then is lovingkindness? It is God's love in covenant enforcement. God begins this discourse on finances and tithing by saying: "I am Jehovah who enforces the covenant and I don't change." Can you see the context in which God wants His people to see their finances and the subject of tithes? He wants His people to see it from a perspective of the covenant and the enforcement of the covenant in their lives.

We must learn to see God's financial plan in the context of the covenant. If it is based on a covenant, then it cannot be activated by God alone. It takes God working with human beings to have the covenant activated on earth. That is why He tells them: "You have departed from My ordinances." In other words, His financial plan was not working for them because they were not doing their part. They were not doing what they needed to do so that He could enforce the covenant in their lives with His power which would fulfil their needs.

Then He says to them: "I do not change." In other words, this is the way it always works.

God has His place in working His plan and human beings have their part in working God's promise even under the New Covenant. God said very plainly: " I am the Lord, I don't change."

Let's look a bit more into the statement: " I am the Lord I change not."

The Hebrew word for "change" here is "shana" and this word also means two, to duplicate, to change and to repeat. There is a lot to unpack in that word "shana" alone.

Remember these verses are addressing the finances of God's people and God is speaking about His financial plan.

God says: "I am the Lord." We have seen that LORD or Jehovah refers to God in exercise of His lovingkindness toward His people in enforcing the covenant.

Remember that a covenant always involves the contribution of at least two parties. God is saying: "I am the Lord I change not." The Hebrew word "shana" also means "two".

We can look at it from this perspective that God is telling His people: "I am the Lord. I am not two. I am one party to the covenant. You are the other party to the covenant. I alone cannot bring about the enforcement of the covenant in your finances. It takes you and me working together to carry it out on earth."

The question is: has that changed today? Has God departed from that plan with the coming in of the new covenant sealed in the blood of Jesus Christ? The answer to that is "no". To fulfil God's word on earth, man has his part to play. God is giving to the people the principles underlying the call to tithes and how it works.

This is what Jesus taught people when He said in Luke 4.21: "And He began to say unto them, today this Scripture is fulfilled in your hearing." In other words, it is fulfilled in faith which comes by hearing the word of God (Rom 10:17). He was telling them they had their part to play in receiving from God.

God gives His people insight into His financial plan by informing them that they had their part to play in it. If they did their part, the plan would work, and their financial needs would be supernaturally and abundantly met and there would be no lack. However, if they departed from doing their part, He would be left alone unable to carry it out in their lives. It works the same today under the new covenant.

Let's look further into the statement: "I am the Lord, I change not."

We have seen that the Hebrew word translated as "change" is "shana" and this word can also mean "two".

Speaking of a person we often say: "That person is dubious." The English word "dubious" originates from the word "duo" meaning "two". When we say someone is dubious, we are therefore saying there are two sides to the person which makes them unreliable and undependable and untrustworthy.

When God says, "I am the Lord I change not", He is saying "I am the God of covenant, and I am the covenant keeping God. That is who I am all the time and will never change. Therefore, you can count on Me."

He highlights the fact that He could be absolutely depended on to keep the covenant where their finances were concerned. They could absolutely trust Him in financial matters.

There are no two faces or sides to God. He does not exhibit one character under the old covenant and then come over to the new covenant and exhibit another. God is consistent in who He is from the old to the new covenant. The same God who prospered His people under the old covenant is the same God of the new covenant. If He is the God of grace in the new covenant, He is the same God of grace under the old covenant. He has not changed. He is not two Gods. Jesus Christ is not another version of God for the new covenant. No, Jesus came to reveal the God of the old covenant perfectly under the new covenant.

In addressing the finances of His people God brings in the concept that He does not change and He is not dubious and can be absolutely relied on to keep the covenant.

He speaks of their finances in the context of the covenant. Hence the financial prosperity of God's people is covenant-prosperity based on God's unchanging nature and character. That must be the way we think of our finances in the new covenant. This concept of covenant- prosperity flows seamlessly from the old to the new covenant.

God told the Israelites the reason for their financial difficulties. It was not because God had changed and was no longer enforcing the covenant. It was because they had abandoned the laws which He gave them to prosper them financially.

We can take comfort that God's plan for our financial success is based on His covenant. If we find out what our part is in this plan and stick to doing it as He has instructed, the guaranteed outcome is that our financial needs will be met through the action of His power.

Psalm 89:34:
"My covenant I will not break,
Nor alter the word that has gone out of My lips."

8

PRESCRIPTION FOR FINANCIAL PROSPERITY

In seeking to gain more insight into God's financial plan for our lives and trying to see if the tithe is part of that plan, we need to track the words that God used in speaking to His covenant people in Malachi 3 and other Scriptures that have to do with the subject. This way our understanding will be enriched, and we can gain a clearer insight into the subject.

God said: "… from the days of your fathers You have gone away from My ordinances" (v 7).

The translation using the word "ordinances" restricts our understanding of the subject because it makes us think in terms of law.

The Hebrew word translated as ordinances here is the Hebrew word "choq" and this word means something prescribed, an enactment, decree, statute, law and rule. It means a prescribed portion or due.

If I were sick and went to the medical doctor for example, he would write a prescription for my condition which I would then take to the pharmacy. That would be the Hebrew concept of "choq".

It would be foolish for me not to take his prescription and expect to get well. If I went back to the doctor with the same condition, the first thing he would do would be to ask me if I took his prescription. If I did not take his prescription, then he couldn't help me.

This is what God was telling His covenant people: "You have gone away from my prescription for your prosperity therefore you have left me out of your finances, and I can't help you in your finances."

God is speaking to them as their prosperity doctor and calling their attention to His prescription to fix their financial problems. He is instructing them how to fix the mess they were in financially. He was not responsible for their financial problems. They had themselves to blame for it. In His mercy toward them He gives them insight into their situation and teaches them the answer for the problem.

The Hebrew word "choq" means "a prescribed portion, prescribed due" and we see this as God gave them His prescription for their continued financial prosperity. He instructed them on what portion of their finances they were to separate from the rest and where to direct it. That prescribed portion was their tithes.

He instructed them to separate this portion as their finances came in and give it to the priest of their time. We shall come back to this again later in our study.

The people departed from His prescription for their financial success and now they were in trouble financially. Then God gives them instruction how to solve problem.

Ecclesiastes 1:9:
"That which has been is what will be,
That which is done is what will be done,
And there is nothing new under the sun."

Financial problems today are not any different from the financial problems people faced under the old covenant. Satan does not have any more new tricks today than he had years ago. It is the same problems that he recycles, and he creates them the same way he did in years gone by. The same principles that God put into operation to solve people's financial problems since the time of Abraham are the same principles available to us today.

DELIVERANCE FROM FINANCIAL DESTRUCTION

Psalm 107:18-20:
"Fools, because of their transgression,
And because of their iniquities, were afflicted.
Their soul abhorred all manner of food,

> And they drew near to the gates of death.
> Then they cried out to the Lord in their trouble,
> And He saved them out of their distresses.
> He sent His word and healed them,
> And delivered them from their destructions."

God had given the people His prescription and if they had followed God's instructions in the first place, He would have kept the destroyer out of their midst, and he (the destroyer) would not have been able to mess up their finances.

God was not to blame for their situation. When we disobey God's word it always opens the door for the devil to get in and create problems in our lives including our finances.

Psalm 107 says: "Fools, because their iniquities and transgression were afflicted." This includes financial affliction. God is not the one afflicting people financially. The Bible says it is because of their iniquities and transgression. In other words, they are not staying with God's instructions.

The Hebrew word translated as "afflicted" means to be tormented, oppressed and poverty. This also includes sickness and disease.

Who is the tormentor as revealed in Scriptures?

Acts 10:38:
> "... how God anointed Jesus of Nazareth with the Holy Spirit and with power, who went about doing good and healing all who were oppressed by the devil, for God was with Him."

Satan is the oppressor and tormentor and when we step out of God's plans as revealed in His word, we open the door for Satan to do his work in our lives.

What did God do? He sent His word to them to deliver them from financial destruction. It is the same today. He has not changed. It is by His word that He delivers us from financial destruction. This is what God was telling the people: "I am the Lord, I change not", which means He does not change in the way He gets things done.

God never forces anything on anybody. Human beings are free moral agents capable of making decision for themselves. We must make the decision to cooperate with God to resolve the issues of our lives including financial problems.

The people had walked away from His financial prescription that guaranteed their financial success and now the destroyer was active in their midst. To resolve their situation, they needed to cooperate with God.

9

GET BACK ON PLAN

Malachi 3:7-8:
"Yet from the days of your fathers
You have gone away from My ordinances
And have not kept them.
Return to Me, and I will return to you,"
Says the Lord of hosts.
"But you said,
'In what way shall we return?'
"Will a man rob God?
Yet you have robbed Me!
But you say,
'In what way have we robbed You?'
In tithes and offerings."

As we track the words that God used in speaking to His people about their finances, we gain insight into how we can cooperate with God to resolve our own financial problems. As the word of God says there is nothing new under the sun.

God told the people to return to Him because He was speaking to them from the standpoint of a covenant relationship. Even though He had the ability to help and deliver them, He could not do it without their cooperation. They had to work with Him. This is why He told them, "return to Me and I will return to you". He was instructing them to get back on plan and they would see His power and presence in their lives including their finances. They would experience His financial turnaround.

The natural question they asked Him was "where do we return to"? In other words, where do we begin?

He answered their question by asking them a question: "Will a man rob God ?"

Again, this word "rob"' is another word that makes a lot of people think of this Scripture in a legalistic way. They say this could not be referring to God's people under the new covenant.

They quote Scriptures like 1 Timothy 1:8-11:

"But we know that the law is good if one uses it lawfully, knowing this: that the law is not made for a righteous person, but for the lawless and insubordinate, for the ungodly and for sinners, for the unholy and profane, for murderers of fathers and murderers of mothers, for manslayers, for fornicators, for sodomites, for kidnappers, for liars, for perjurers, and if there is any other thing that is contrary to sound doctrine, according to the glorious gospel of the blessed God which was committed to my trust."

However, God was not trying to bring the people under condemnation by saying, "you have robbed me". He wants them to see the source of their financial problems so they could cooperate with Him to resolve it.

Let's look at this word "rob" which God used in these verses. The Hebrew word is "qaba" and this word means to "limit" or to "'fix something or someone in a particular position".

Do you see why God asked them the question, "will a man rob God"? In other words, "will man limit or have God fixed where He is unable to act on their behalf?"

Their thinking about God then is no different from the average person's thinking about God today. They were thinking God is sovereign and omnipotent which is true.

Their thinking was that mere human beings could never in any way limit or have God in a position where He is unable to move on their behalf in anything. This is how we tend to think about God today and God is correcting that notion by telling us that this is exactly what we are doing to Him.

It is true that God is sovereign and omnipotent, but God also keeps His word. He cannot break His word.

Let us look at what the word of God has to say in this regard:

Genesis 1:26-27:
"Then God said, 'Let Us make man in Our image, according to Our likeness; let them have dominion over the fish of the sea, over the birds of the air, and over the cattle, over all the earth and over every creeping thing that creeps on the earth.' So God created man in His own image; in the image of God He created him; male and female He created them."

God created man and placed him in dominion here on earth. That means God gave human beings authority over the planet earth. He would not turn around and brush aside that authority and arbitrarily do whatever He wants to do here on earth. No! God has to work with and through people to accomplish His will on earth. People have to cooperate with Him.

Through the prophet Malachi God was helping them to understand the situation so they could cooperate with Him to resolve it. They were limiting Him through their disobedience. By moving away from his financial plan, they had left Him on the outside where He could not do much for them. Doesn't that principle apply today under the new covenant?

We have seen that the Hebrew word translated "to rob", "qaba", means "to fix something in a position". When you are fixed you are unable to move. The natural human mind cannot fathom this that human beings can have God in a position where is He is unable to move on their behalf. This is because by His word God has placed man in dominion on earth and He cannot violate His word. When they stopped cooperating with Him according to His word, He was unable to move in their finances and the devil had it all to himself to destroy them financially.

Ephesians 3.20:

"Now to Him who is able to do exceedingly abundantly above all that we ask or think, according to the power that works in us, to Him be glory in the church by Christ Jesus to all generations, forever and ever."

I really love the literal Greek translation of this verse which says:

"Now to the one being able beyond all things to do superabundantly of which we ask or think according to the power operating in us ..."

God's ability is beyond all things to do! In other words, there is no situation you can be in financially or other areas of life that God's power cannot turn around. Whatever your financial situation is like today, however much indebted you are, God can resolve it for you supernaturally, but He needs your cooperation.

Notice it says: "... according to the power operating in us ..." The operation of His power is subject to human beings on earth.

God does not switch on or switch off His power arbitrarily. The switch to God's power on earth is faith. It is human beings that control this switch of faith. We can with our words and actions switch off the operation of His power in our lives and circumstances or we can switch it on by faith to work on our behalf to meet our needs.

This is the understanding God was getting across to the people in Malachi 3 and it is applicable to us today under the new covenant.

Psalm 78:40-41:

"How often they provoked Him in the wilderness, And grieved Him in the desert! Yes, again and again they tempted God, And limited the Holy One of Israel."

Yes, it is human beings that limit what God can do in their personal lives by thinking and acting out of line with His word. This is why God wants our thinking renewed so that we think in line with what He says in His word so that His power can work unhindered in all areas of our lives including our finances.

When God told them they were robbing Him it was not to get them under condemnation but to let them know that they were hindering Him from moving freely on their behalf especially in their financial affairs and He showed them how they could cooperate with Him to resolve the problem. That principle is applicable to us today even in the new covenant.

Matthew 13:54-58:

"When He had come to His own country, He taught them in their synagogue, so that they were astonished and said, 'Where did this Man get this wisdom and these mighty works? Is this not the carpenter's son? Is not His mother called Mary? And His brothers James, Joses, Simon, and Judas? And His sisters, are they not all with us? Where then did this Man get all these things?' So they were offended at Him. But Jesus said to them, 'A prophet is not without honor except in his own country and in his own house.' Now He did not do many mighty works there because of their unbelief."

We can see the same problem at work in the ministry of Jesus Christ the Son of God when He was on earth in His hometown. He preached the same message to them that He had preached elsewhere with great results and miracles. In His hometown they wouldn't receive His message. The Bible says: "He did not do many mighty works there ..." It does not say He was unwilling to do mighty works and miracles. He was willing to do the same mighty works He had done elsewhere but He could not do them in His hometown because of their unbelief.

Their unbelief kept that power from working for them. All He could do was heal a few sick folks. Another translation says He healed a few with minor ailments. This is a typical case of human beings limiting what God could do in their midst and this is what God was telling the people through the prophet Malachi.

We have however seen this Hebrew word "qaba" mostly in terms of robbing God and we have not got the full significance of what God was saying to the people.

Once we see that God was telling them they were limiting Him we can see how it applies to us today. We can see how by not cooperating with God and following His plans for our finances we can severely limit what He can do with His power in our lives and circumstances, and we can even have Him in a place where He is unable to move on our behalf.

10

TITHING AND YOUR FINANCES

God gives voice through the prophet to the question that would naturally come to mind: "Wherein have we robbed you?"

We have seen that the Hebrew word translated as "rob" expanded in our understanding. The word means to limit and fix. The people were asking God, "where have we limited and had you fixed, where you are unable to move in our affairs?" Then God identifies it to them. He said to them: "In tithes and offerings".

God was telling them: "Your tithes and offerings have everything to do with taking the limits off Me and releasing Me to move on your behalf."

Therefore, we can see that tithes do have a place in God's financial plan for His people.

This fact we can see clearly as far as the Old Testament is concerned but does the tithe have any place in God's financial plan for His people under the new covenant?

Let's allow the Holy Spirit to guide us through Scripture into the answer to this question.

God said to His people to get back on plan. How?

He said to them in Malachi 3:10-11:

> "'Bring all the tithes into the storehouse,
> That there may be food in My house,
> And try Me now in this,'
> Says the Lord of hosts,
> 'If I will not open for you the windows of heaven
> And pour out for you such blessing
> That there will not be room enough to receive it.

> And I will rebuke the devourer for your sakes,
> So that he will not destroy the fruit of your ground,
> Nor shall the vine fail to bear fruit for you in the field,'
> Says the Lord of hosts."

He instructs His covenant people to bring all the tithes into the storehouse and in so doing they would be back on plan with Him again and He would be free to move in their financial affairs.

At this point let's take a pause to answer another simple but important question.

WHAT IS THE TITHE?

This seems to be an unnecessary question because the answer seems to be self-evident.

The tithe has been defined as ten percent of our income. But is that all there is to the tithe?

Looking at the way God taught Israel to practice the tithe there is more to the tithe than just ten percent.

> **Genesis 14:17-20:**
> "And the king of Sodom went out to meet him at the Valley of Shaveh (that is, the King's Valley), after his return from the defeat of Chedorlaomer and the kings who were with him. Then Melchizedek king of Salem brought out bread and wine; he was the priest of God Most High.
> And he blessed him and said:
> 'Blessed be Abram of God Most High,
> Possessor of heaven and earth;
> And blessed be God Most High,
> Who has delivered your enemies into your hand.'
> And he gave him a tithe of all."

The Scripture above is the first place where the practice of tithing is mentioned in the entire Bible.

By paying attention into how it was practiced here we gain more insight into the meaning of the tithe.

In the passage above it says Abraham gave Melchizedek tithes of all. The Hebrew word translated as tithes is "maaser". This means a tenth alright, but it is " the tenth that completes or concludes a unit of ten." Or it can be put this way: "the concluding or completing tenth".

The way Abraham did it here was to take the spoils of war and separate them into units of ten and each tenth of part of a unit of ten was separated unto God. This was a meticulous process and God had them do it this way to convey revelation to His people concerning the role of the tithe in their finances.

Hold the definition of the tithe as "the concluding or completing tenth" in your mind as we go along.

Let's gain more insight into our understanding of the tithe as God instructed the Israelites to practice it under the old covenant.

Leviticus 27:32-33:

"And concerning the tithe of the herd or the flock, of whatever passes under the rod, the tenth one shall be holy to the Lord. He shall not inquire whether it is good or bad, nor shall he exchange it; and if he exchanges it at all, then both it and the one exchanged for it shall be holy; it shall not be redeemed.'"

The Israelites at this time were essentially an agricultural society mostly farming the land and keeping flocks of cattle. Now in this Scripture the Lord instructs the shepherds among them how to separate the tithe from their flocks.

The shepherd herded the flock into a pen and made a small opening for them in the pen. This opening was only big enough to allow one sheep through at a time. Then with his shepherd's rod held out over them he counted them as they passed through this opening. One, two, three, four, five, six, seven, eight, nine and then as the tenth one came, the shepherd marked it with a red stripe and declared "this is the tithe!".

Through this process God taught them to see in the tithe something beyond just ten percent.

He was communicating to His people through the practice of separating the tenth in a unit of ten, the revelation of the place the tithe held in His financial plan for them.

Maaser or the tithe was "the concluding tenth or the completing tenth".

It was much the same way with the harvest from their fields. The harvest was gathered in stacks or bundles and as they carried the stacks away from the field of harvest, they counted them much the same way with the flock and every tenth bundle of the harvest was declared "maaser" or the tithe.

The inspired writer of the book of Hebrews confirms this practice to us in talking about Abraham's tithes to Melchizedek.

Hebrews 7:1-2:
"For this Melchizedek, king of Salem, priest of the Most High God, who met Abraham returning from the slaughter of the kings and blessed him, to whom also Abraham gave a tenth part of all, first being translated 'king of righteousness', and then also king of Salem, meaning 'king of peace'."

The literal translation gives us the picture of Abraham separating the tenth part of a series of ten portions and handing it over to Melchizedek.

Hebrews 7:5:
"And indeed those who are of the sons of Levi, who receive the priesthood, have a commandment to receive tithes from the people according to the law, that is, from their brethren, though they have come from the loins of Abraham."

Here we see the commandment to the Levitical Priesthood to take the tithes from the people.

The word used here is "apodekato" which is from two words "apo" which means to take out from or away from or to separate from. Then we have the word "dekato" which is from the Greek word "ten". Put together the words mean "to separate the tenth in a unit of ten". This is why the tithe came to be seen as " the concluding tenth" or "the tenth that completes".

How does this tie up with finances?

Look at the word "finance". The English word for finance is from an old word which means "to finish, to end or to settle". You can also look at it from the Hebrew perspective. The Hebrew word "to pay" is also from the root word "shalom" which means to complete or to be complete or make whole.

For example if you were buying a house that transaction is completed or finished when money changes hands from you the buyer to the owner of the property. If payment is not made the transaction is not yet completed or we could say the house is not yet financed. If you did not have the money to make the full payments on that house, you would then look for a third party like a bank to lend you the money to complete that transaction and so we say, "the bank financed the purchase of that property".

God was telling them "the tithe is involved in their finances because it is the completing or concluding tenth portion". The tithe is the tenth that brings " financial peace".

We miss what God is communicating to us when we just define the tithe as ten percent and that is why we argue whether it is for us in the new covenant. By paying attention to the way the Israelites practiced the tithe, we get the revelation behind it, and we see that God was teaching His people to see their finances in terms of the tithe.

11

PRINCIPLES AND PRACTICE

Now we have seen some details into how God instructed Israel to practice the tithe.

As we see Israel practice tithing as God instructed, we get a revelation that the tithe is much more than just giving ten percent of our income, it is part of our financial peace or wholeness. The Hebrew word for peace means "nothing broken, nothing missing". If you are broke, in debt and unable to pay your bills, that does not look like financial peace, does it?

We must realise some practices may be different between the Old and New Testaments, but God's principles are the same throughout the bible. Principles don't change.

The way Israel practiced the tithe under the Old Testament is not necessarily the way it is to be practiced in the new covenant, but the principle of the tithe is the same in the old and new Testaments. However, as we study the way Israel practiced the tithe under the old covenant, we draw revelation knowledge that reinforces the practice of it in the new covenant. This is how we can see that the tithe is part of God's financial wholeness or peace plan.

Romans 15:4:
"For whatever things were written before were written for our learning, that we through the patience and comfort of the Scriptures might have hope."

Whatever was written before includes all that was written about the tithe in the Scriptures most especially under the old covenant. The Bible says it should produce patience in us and how does that happen? By reinforcing our understanding.

The principle of the tithe remains constant because principles are timeless. They don't change but the practices may be different from the Old to the New Testament.

One of the examples of the way principles remain constant where practices differ is in worship. The principles that govern worship are the same whether in the old covenant or in new covenant.

This is what Jesus was communicating to the Samaritan woman at the well.

> **John 4:19-24:**
>
> **"The woman said to Him, 'Sir, I perceive that You are a prophet. Our fathers worshiped on this mountain, and you Jews say that in Jerusalem is the place where one ought to worship.'**
>
> **"Jesus said to her, 'Woman, believe Me, the hour is coming when you will neither on this mountain, nor in Jerusalem, worship the Father. You worship what you do not know; we know what we worship, for salvation is of the Jews. But the hour is coming, and now is, when the true worshipers will worship the Father in spirit and truth; for the Father is seeking such to worship Him. God is Spirit, and those who worship Him must worship in spirit and truth.'"**

Under the old covenant worship was centralised to where the temple was in Jerusalem. The Samaritans however believed that worship should be centralised at mount Gerizim.

Jesus then teaches her that the time had come for a change in the practice from the Old Testament practice of worshipping God in a physical location to the New Testament practice of worshipping God in spirit and truth. The principles governing worship however remain constant whether in the old or in new covenant.

In Malachi 3:6-12 God is instructing His people on the principles that undergird the practice of tithing.

This is why He begins by declaring: " I am the Lord I change not." His principles are consistent with His character. He does not change and therefore His principles do not change.

The practice of worship has changed from the old to the new covenant because human beings will now receive the life and nature of God into their spirits making it possible to contact God in the spirit unlike the old covenant when worshippers were spiritually dead.

It is the same with the tithe. Israel practiced it differently under Old Testament, but the principle of the tithe remains the same from the old to the new covenant.

For example, God prescribed three different kinds of tithes under the old covenant and even specified what kind of agricultural produce they should tithe. That practice is however limited to God's Old Testament people. We have no specific instructions to do tithing in this way under the new covenant which would be impossible to do anyway because we live in a more diversified type of economy where not everybody is a farmer or sheep breeder.

However, the principle remains the same that the tithe is in God's financial plan for us, and God wants us to see our finances in terms of the tithe. God is teaching us kingdom finance in terms of the tithe.

Matthew 6:33:
"But seek first the kingdom of God and His righteousness, and all these things shall be added to you."

FINANCIAL PRINCIPLES OF GOD'S WISDOM

Practices may change but principles don't change. Principles govern all areas of life. God's financial principles are timeless because they belong in the realm of His wisdom.

Proverbs 4:7:
"Wisdom is the principal thing;
Therefore get wisdom.

And in all your getting, get understanding."

The word principal and principle are practically the same words. In this Scripture it simply means that God's wisdom is the master principle for all life and if we are going to master living, we are going to have to tap the wisdom of God.

In the area of our finances, if we are going to gain financial mastery, we must tap God's Kingdom financial principles.

He gave those principles to Israel under the old covenant and when Israel walked in God's financial principles, they became the head of the nations of the world financially. Those principles are unchanging and remain the same today even under the new covenant.

Proverbs 8:6:
"Listen, for I will speak of excellent things, And from the opening of my lips will come right things."

The phrase "excellent things" translated from the Hebrew Bible can be translated "I will speak princes". In other words, when wisdom speaks "princes come out her mouth".

The Hebrew word used here is from the root word "nagid" which means "prince".

The English word for principle and principal ultimately come from the same word "prince" or "chief". Hence, when God says all His words are "nagid" it simply means all His utterances are principles of life.

Just as the universe is governed by laws and principles so the utterances of wisdom are principles of life. Practices may change but principles don't change.

We can extend that to the subject of tithing. It is first and foremost a financial principle of God's kingdom and then God adapted it to the practices of Israel under the old covenant.

The old covenant may have passed away with the death and resurrection of Jesus Christ, but God's principles of wisdom did not pass away. They are eternal.

The word "principle" means "one who takes first part". Hence, when God speaks, we ought to give His word first place in our lives which is what wisdom is all about. A wise man pays attention to God's word and gives it first place in all areas of life including finances.

If we really want to turn our financial situations around God's way, we have to start paying attention to God's timeless financial principles and start putting them to work in our daily living.

The Webster's Ninth New Collegiate dictionary says principle means "a comprehensive and fundamental law, doctrine, or assumption. It means a rule of law or conduct. It means a primary source or origin".

When we gain understanding of the principles of God regarding the subject of healing and health, we have tapped into the source of all health. When we gain understanding of the principles of God's wisdom in finances, we have tapped into the source of all financial success. The tithe is a divine principle of financial success.

Genesis 14:18-23:
"Then Melchizedek king of Salem brought out bread and wine; he was the priest of God Most High. And he blessed him and said:
'Blessed be Abram of God Most High,
Possessor of heaven and earth;
And blessed be God Most High,
Who has delivered your enemies into your hand.'
And he gave him a tithe of all.
Now the king of Sodom said to Abram, 'Give me the persons, and take the goods for yourself.'

But Abram said to the king of Sodom, 'I have raised my hand to the Lord, God Most High, the Possessor of heaven and earth, that I will take nothing, from a thread to a sandal strap, and that I will not take anything that is yours, lest you should say, 'I have made Abram rich.'"

Abraham, in this first mention of tithing in the whole Bible had tapped into the financial principles of God's wisdom and was able to look to God exclusively as His source. Nobody would be able to take credit for his financial success.

The principle of tithing was part of Abraham's financial success and God's principles are timeless.

THE FOUNDATION OF PRINCIPLES

Jesus likened the doer of God's word to a wise man who dug deep and built his house on the rock.

> **Luke 6:48:**
> **"He is like a man building a house, who dug deep and laid the foundation on the rock. And when the flood arose, the stream beat vehemently against that house, and could not shake it, for it was founded on the rock."**

This man went beyond the practice of what people were doing and found the underlying principle in the word and based his actions on the principle because he understood principles will work the same way all the time. That is what made him wise.

Undergirding the practices of tithing under the old covenant is the timeless principle of God's wisdom which should work just as well in the New Testament. In fact, it should work better under this dispensation because we live under a new and better covenant in Christ Jesus.

12

THE RULE OF FIRST MENTION

It is true that the New Testament appears silent on the tithe. For example, the word "tithe" is mentioned fourteen times from the Old to the New Testament and out of those fourteen times only two of them occur in the New Testament. Then the word "tithes" occurs twenty-three times between the Old and New Testament and out of these it occurs only five times in the New Testament. The word "tithing" occurs only two times in the Bible and both these occurrences occur in the Old Testament.

When we take the words "tithe", "tithes" and "tithing" together they occur a total of thirty-nine times in the entire Bible and out of these they occur only seven times in the New Testament. That represents approximately 18 percent of the total occurrences in the Bible.

Many argue that this is an indication that tithing is not relevant to the New Testament church.

Is this argument correct and what is the reason for the relative silence of the New Testament on this subject?

The Lord Jesus Christ in His teaching and discourses is documented to have mentioned tithes twice (Matt 23:23 which is restated in Luke 11.42 and Luke 18.12).

The key to understanding the reason for this apparent silence is in the law of first mention in Biblical interpretation.

E.W. Bullinger in his book *How to Enjoy the Bible*, lists twelve canons or rules for Biblical interpretation. The canon or rule of first mention is cited as canon five among these twelve canons.

Bullinger states this rule or canon as follows: "The first occurrence of words, expressions, and utterances are generally essential to their interpretation."

He further states in explaining this canon or rule: "This is a law we have long since noticed and have never yet found to fail. The first occurrence of a word, or an expression, or an utterance is the key to its subsequent usage and meaning; or at least a guide as to the essential point connected with it."

Let us apply this canon or rule to our understanding of the tithe and see if it explains why the Lord Jesus Christ and New Testament writers are largely silent on it.

The first occurrence of the word "tithe" is in Genesis 14:16-17:

> **"So he brought back all the goods, and also brought back his brother Lot and his goods, as well as the women and the people.**
> **"And the king of Sodom went out to meet him at the Valley of Shaveh (that is, the King's Valley), after his return from the defeat of Chedorlaomer and the kings who were with him."**

Abraham had just returned victorious from a battle against a coalition of armies from different nation states at that time who had taken his nephew Lot captive.

For the first time we see the mention of a mysterious figure called Melchizedek meeting with Abraham.

Melchizedek blesses Abraham who at this time was still referred to as "Abram". He attributes Abraham's victory in warfare to God most High and then the Bible says: "Abram gave him tithe of all."

This is the first time the tithe is mentioned in the whole of Scripture. One very important point that stands out here is that the law is not mentioned but it says concerning this mysterious figure called Melchizedek that "He was the Priest of God Most high".

The first time the subject of tithing is mentioned in the Bible is in connection with the priesthood of Melchizedek.

In line with the rule or canon of first mention, this fact of mentioning the tithe in connection with the priesthood of Melchizedek should guide our minds when we look at every occurrence of tithe, tithes and tithing in Scriptures. Doing this will help us understand why the New Testament seems largely silent on the subject.

Let us follow this canon or rule of interpretation through the Old Testament and see how it works out.

The first time the tithe is mentioned under the law is in Leviticus 27:30:

"And all the tithe of the land, whether of the seed of the land or of the fruit of the tree, is the Lord's. It is holy to the Lord."

It is mentioned first in the law under the ministry or office of the Levitical Priesthood consistent with the law of first mention in Genesis 14:16-20.

Notice that the first mention of the tithe in the entire bible is in the book of Genesis and it is in connection with a priesthood which is the priesthood of Melchizedek.

Its first mention under the law of Moses was in connection with a priesthood which is the Levitical Priesthood headed by Aaron. The common factor here is priesthood. Don't lose sight of this fact.

Hebrews 7:5 alludes to this:

"And indeed those who are of the sons of Levi, who receive the priesthood, have a commandment to receive tithes from the people according to the law, that is, from their brethren, though they have come from the loins of Abraham."

It is mentioned here that the Levitical priesthood was divinely mandated to collect the tithes under the old covenant and so its first mention with the giving of the law of Moses is in the book of Leviticus.

We can see this canon or rule 5 of Bible interpretation according to E. W. Bullinger holding firm so far.

Reading through the other portions of the instructions of God to the people through Moses we see that the tithe was always mentioned in connection with the priesthood of Levi.

Numbers 18:24:

"For the tithes of the children of Israel, which they offer up as a heave offering to the Lord, I have given to the Levites as an inheritance; therefore I have said to them, 'Among the children of Israel they shall have no inheritance.'"

You can look up the other references to tithes from Exodus and all the way to Deuteronomy and you will see that the priesthood is always mentioned in connection with tithes. This is consistent with the rule of first mention which begins with Genesis 14:16-20.

Priesthood therefore and not the Law of Moses is fundamental to our understanding of the tithe from the Old Testament to the New Testament.

Let us look beyond the law to another aspect of the Old Testament. The Old Testament is commonly referred to by Jews as the TANACH. That is because of their division of all the books of the Old Testament into three basic sections which make up the acronym TANACH.

TANAKH is an acronym derived from the following words Torah, (which stands for the first five books of the Bible referred to as the Chumash), Nevim which refers to the prophets and the Ketuvim which means writings.

Jesus Christ, however, in His discourses referred to the Old Testament in two broad sections: the law and the prophets.

Matthew 22:37-40:

"Jesus said to him, 'You shall love the Lord your God with all your heart, with all your soul, and with all your mind. This is the first and great commandment. And the second is like it: You shall love your neighbor as yourself.' On these two commandments hang all the Law and the Prophets."

That means according to Jesus Christ if it is outside of the law, that mention of tithing would fall under the prophets.

Now let's examine the tithes in the prophets according to rule or canon of first mention.

> **2 Chronicles 31:4-5:**
>
> **"Moreover he commanded the people who dwelt in Jerusalem to contribute support for the priests and the Levites, that they might devote themselves to the Law of the Lord."**

As soon as the commandment was circulated, the children of Israel brought in abundance the firstfruits of grain and wine, oil and honey, and of all the produce of the field; and they brought in abundantly the tithe of everything."

Here we see the first mention of tithe outside of the law in what would come under the prophets in the teaching of Jesus Christ. Again, we see it is being mentioned in connection with the priesthood. This is consistent with the rule or canon of first mention which we have been tracking all the way from Genesis 14:16-20.

We can find other Scriptures in this regard in the following places: 2 Chronicles 31:12, Nehemiah 10:37-38, Nehemiah 13:12, Nehemiah 12:44, and Nehemiah 13:5. In all these Scriptures we find the rule or canon of first mention holds firm throughout.

Then we have what appears to be a strange Scripture which does not appear to fit into this rule in Amos 4:4:

> **"Come to Bethel and transgress,**
> **At Gilgal multiply transgression;**
> **Bring your sacrifices every morning,**
> **Your tithes every three days".**

It would seem as if God was speaking of a different kind of tithe here to be offered every three days, but the Hebrew translation of "days" is "yamim" and this word also means years. Hence, it is speaking of the three yearly charity tithe also called "maaser ani" which was generally to be given to the poor and foreigners within their communities. This tithe was also administered under the supervision of the Levitical Priesthood.

Then we come to the Old Testament's most famous tithing verses and perhaps the most contentious.

Malachi 3:10:
"'Bring all the tithes into the storehouse,
That there may be food in My house,
And try Me now in this,'
Says the Lord of hosts,
'If I will not open for you the windows of heaven
And pour out for you such blessing
That there will not be room enough to receive it.'"

It says bring all the tithes into my storehouse. Where is this storehouse which this Scripture speaks about? The Hebrew Bible says: " Bayit Ha owtsar", which literarily means " house of the storehouse". God was saying to the people bring all the tithes into "the house of the storehouse". What does this mean? Where is the " house of the storehouse?"

We see from Scriptures that the storehouse was in the temple, and this storehouse was created during the second temple era to accommodate the excess of the tithes and offerings of God's people.

Nehemiah 12:44:
"And at the same time some were appointed over the rooms of the storehouse for the offerings, the firstfruits, and the tithes, to gather into them from the fields of the cities the portions specified by the Law for the priests and Levites; for Judah rejoiced over the priests and Levites who ministered."

Therefore, we can see that " the storehouse" was in the temple which was where the Levitical Priesthood worked and ministered from.

We see again the rule or canon of first mention which we have been tracking from Genesis 14.16-20 holding firm in the great tithing Scripture of the Old Testament which also happens to be the last mention of it before the gospel era that began with Jesus Christ.

As we look at the tithe considering this rule of interpretation called the rule of first mention, we gain a greater and balanced understanding of the tithe and can begin to get insight into why the Lord Jesus seemed to be silent on it and why much of the New Testament is also silent on it. It is not because the tithe is any less important in the New Testament than it was under the Old Testament.

13

TRANSITION TO A NEW PRIESTHOOD

The period in which the Lord Jesus Christ ministered was a transition period. It was generally a transition from one covenant to another and one priesthood to another priesthood.

As we study the teachings and statements of Jesus Christ, we generally will see this transition reflected in His words.

The sun was setting on the old covenant dispensation with its law, temple, priesthood and sacrifices and the dawn of a new covenant dispensation with a new priesthood, a new law and change in the mode of worship was on the horizon.

The Person by whom this change would come about was the Lord Jesus Christ Himself.

This is the reason why Jesus Christ Himself spoke very little about the tithe in His teachings and discourses.

We have basically three references in the gospels where the Lord Jesus Christ spoke about the tithe and in these Scriptures, it was in a spirit of rebuke to the religious hypocrites of the day who had lost sight of God's intention for giving the law and were more preoccupied with what merits they could earn from God for their good works in keeping the law.

However, suffice to know for now that the reason Jesus was largely silent on the tithe was because the priesthood was then about to pass away with the old covenant sealed in the blood of bulls and goats.

John 16:12-14:
"I still have many things to say to you, but you cannot bear them now. However, when He, the Spirit of truth, has come,

He will guide you into all truth; for He will not speak on His own authority, but whatever He hears He will speak; and He will tell you things to come. He will glorify Me, for He will take of what is Mine and declare it to you."

Telling them that the Levitical Priesthood headed by Aaron and his descendants was about to pass away with the covenant under which they lived and that in a short while they would not have to take their tithes and offerings to the priests that officiated at that time, were truths which they could not handle yet. Those were truths reserved for a new dispensation on the horizon under which the Holy Spirit would dwell in the hearts of people and from within guide them into all truth.

THE TITHE AND THE RULE OF FIRST MENTION IN THE NEW COVENANT

We have seen the words tithe, tithes and tithing are used a total of 39 times in the entire Bible out of which they occur only seven times in the New Testament.

However, this statement is not very accurate because we have included Matthew, Mark, Luke and John under the new covenant which in a legal technical sense is not correct.

The reason is that while Jesus ministered on earth, the record of which is captured in the four gospels, the new covenant was not legally in operation before His death on the cross.

Hebrews 9:15-16:
"And for this reason He is the Mediator of the new covenant, by means of death, for the redemption of the transgressions under the first covenant, that those who are called may receive the promise of the eternal inheritance. For where there is a testament, there must also of necessity be the death of the testator."

This Scripture tells us that the death of Jesus was necessary to bring the new covenant into force. That means while He lived and walked in the land of Israel the new covenant was not yet in operation.

Jesus, while He was on earth, ministered as a prophet under the old covenant.

Galatians 4:4-5:
"But when the fullness of the time had come, God sent forth His Son, born of a woman, born under the law, to redeem those who were under the law, that we might receive the adoption as sons."

Jesus lived and ministered under the Law of Moses until He went to the cross and shed His blood, dying there to bring the law to an end and begin a new covenant dispensation.

In the light of this, the instances of the mention of the tithe by Jesus Christ should not be counted under the new covenant. They should be counted under the old covenant. We shall study those statements of Jesus Christ in the gospels later.

For now, in tracking the rule or canon of first mention of the tithe into the New Testament we should begin not in the gospels but in the epistles because the new covenant dispensation began in the book of Acts and then into the epistles.

The first mention of the subject of tithe in the New Testament is therefore in the book of Hebrews, and what is the main subject under discussion in the book of Hebrews? It is emergence of a New High Priest and a new covenant in the Person of Jesus Christ.

Hebrews 3:1:
"Therefore, holy brethren, partakers of the heavenly calling, consider the Apostle and High Priest of our confession, Christ Jesus."

This is the first time in the entire epistles that the revelation of Jesus Christ as Hight Priest mediating a new covenant is revealed.

It is in this same epistle that we see the subject of the tithe mentioned for the first time.

Hebrews 7:1-3

"For this Melchizedek, king of Salem, priest of the Most High God, who met Abraham returning from the slaughter of the kings and blessed him, to whom also Abraham gave a tenth part of all, first being translated 'king of righteousness,' and then also king of Salem, meaning 'king of peace,' without father, without mother, without genealogy, having neither beginning of days nor end of life, but made like the Son of God, remains a priest continually.'"

All other epistles of the new covenant are silent about tithes and tithing because the revelation of the priesthood of Jesus Christ was not yet available to the church.

The Holy Spirit through the apostles of the church did not give any instructions to the churches to tithe because any such instructions on tithes and tithing would have been inappropriate.

Can you see the reason for the silence now? It was an inspired silence on the part of the Holy Spirit.

When we study the book of Acts, we see the early church was still largely in the dark as to the full significance of the death, burial, and resurrection of Jesus. They had no idea of what He had ascended to the Father to do.

Acts 1:6-8:

"Therefore, when they had come together, they asked Him, saying, 'Lord, will You at this time restore the kingdom to Israel?' And He said to them, 'It is not for you to know times or seasons which the Father has put in His own authority. But you shall receive power when the Holy Spirit has come upon

you; and you shall be witnesses to Me in Jerusalem, and in all Judea and Samaria, and to the end of the earth.'"

They were still at this time thinking that His resurrection would bring about the end of Rome's domination of their land and bring about the restoration of the glory of the physical kingdom of Israel.

These were Jews who had been brought up under the Levitical Priesthood and they had taken their tithes and offering all their lives to the officiating priests in the temple that was still standing. To instruct them to give tithes would mean asking them to take those tithes to a priesthood that had come to an end with the death of Jesus Christ at the cross. That would mean affirming a Levitical Priesthood which was already dead as far as God was concerned. This is why we do not see any form of instruction regarding tithing in the book of Acts. The people gave as the Spirit of God directed them to give.

Acts 4:32-36:
"Now the multitude of those who believed were of one heart and one soul; neither did anyone say that any of the things he possessed was his own, but they had all things in common.
And with great power the apostles gave witness to the resurrection of the Lord Jesus. And great grace was upon them all. Nor was there anyone among them who lacked; for all who were possessors of lands or houses sold them, and brought the proceeds of the things that were sold, and laid them at the apostles' feet; and they distributed to each as anyone had need.
"And Joses, who was also named Barnabas by the apostles (which is translated Son of Encouragement), a Levite of the country of Cyprus, having land, sold it, and brought the money and laid it at the apostles' feet."

There is no mention here of the early church practicing tithing because the revelation of the New Priesthood of Jesus Christ had not yet come to them.

When we study Paul's instructions to the churches concerning giving, he did not mention tithing and the reason for this is very clear in the light of the rule of first mention about tithes. In the epistles we find no mention of the Priesthood of Jesus Christ except in the epistle to the Hebrews. There is a Holy Spirit inspired silence about tithing from the book of Acts right into the epistles until we come into the epistle to the Hebrews and then the subject of tithing is opened.

In the book of Hebrews, the inspired silence regarding the place of tithes in God's financial plan for the New Testament believers is broken for the first time as Jesus Christ the High Priest of a better covenant is now revealed.

14

THE TITHE: LAW OR GRACE?

Many argue that tithe belongs under the law and that Jesus Christ brought the law dispensation to an end and in so doing brought the practice of tithing to an end and as such the church is not under obligation to practice tithing.

They quote Scriptures like Romans 10:4:

> **"For Christ is the end of the law for righteousness to everyone who believes."**

However, the key to understanding the spirit and intention behind the tithe is not the law of Moses but the priesthood. Therefore, to be able to say whether the tithe belongs under law or grace we need to see the difference between law and priesthood.

The law makes us aware of our sinfulness and guilt before the justice of God.

> **Romans 3:19-20:**
> **"Now we know that whatever the law says, it says to those who are under the law, that every mouth may be stopped, and all the world may become guilty before God. Therefore by the deeds of the law no flesh will be justified in His sight, for by the law is the knowledge of sin."**

Then we learn further that the law brings about the wrath of God.

> **Romans 4:15:**
> **"… because the law brings about wrath; for where there is no law there is no transgression."**

Furthermore, the law confirms the dominion of sin over sinful human beings.

> **Romans 6:14:**
> "For sin shall not have dominion over you, for you are not under law but under grace."

Then again, the law causes the sinfulness of fallen human beings to be active, working to produce death.

> **Romans 7:13:**
> "Has then what is good become death to me? Certainly not! But sin, that it might appear sin, was producing death in me through what is good, so that sin through the commandment might become exceedingly sinful."

The law causes people to become more aware of their failings, their sinfulness and guilt and works condemnation in them therefore the law cannot bring about faith in God.

> **Galatians 3:11-12:**
> "But that no one is justified by the law in the sight of God is evident, for 'the just shall live by faith.' Yet the law is not of faith, but 'the man who does them shall live by them.'"
>
> "The law was the full, comprehensive and profound commentary on the consequences of the Fall. It revealed to the Jew man's deep-seated estrangement from God, his depravity and corruption, the sinfulness of the very root and fountain of our life. The holiness of God and man's sin and sinfulness were thus vividly impressed on God's ancient people"
> (Adolph Saphir, 1875).

In light of the above it is obvious that the law exposes and reinforces the rift between a righteous and Holy God and fallen, sinful human beings making it impossible for God to do anything good for him other than pour out His judgment and wrath on him.

Priesthood however speaks of mediation between God and sinful man. Priesthood seeks forgiveness for sinful man and works to bring about reconciliation. Without the mediation of a priesthood, it was impossible for a Holy and just God to enter a covenant relationship of blessing with sinful man. So, while the law activates the curse on sinful man , the priesthood seeks to keep the curse out and usher in God's blessings on sinful human beings.

The law confirms sinful man in broken fellowship while priesthood brings man back into communion with God, bringing to man the love of God and returning to God the worship and service of man.

The law brings upon sinful human beings that which they deserve which is judgement, wrath, and punishment. Priesthood brings to human beings that which they don't deserve which is grace. The priesthood is the foundation for God's grace.

Since the tithe came to us not through law but in the context of priesthood, we can safely conclude, based on the rule of first mention, that the tithe belongs in grace.

The revelation of the tithe came from God to His people in a spirit of grace.

The tithe belongs under grace not law.

What is grace? It is God's willingness to use His power on our behalf as human beings even though we don't deserve it.

God wants to use His power to meet our needs and move on our behalf in the financial realm even though we deserve to be poor and go without our needs being met according to our works.

God wants to get into covenant partnership with us in the financial realm so that we can be blessed and be a blessing while we are in this world.

Grace empowers us to be tithers and as we tithe God can move powerfully on our behalf in the financial realm.

This is the Spirit behind Jacob's vow in Genesis 28:20-22:

> **"Then Jacob made a vow, saying, 'If God will be with me, and keep me in this way that I am going, and give me bread to eat and clothing to put on, so that I come back to my father's house in peace, then the Lord shall be my God. And this stone which I have set as a pillar shall be God's house, and of all that You give me I will surely give a tenth to You.'"**

He pledged the tithe up front knowing that without God's enablement he could not do it. That is the spirit of grace. Faith says: " I can do it only by divine enablement …" Faith says: " it is God that is at work in me to will and to do His good pleasure."

Faith says: "God in exercise of His grace puts on my hands the tithe seed and by His enablement I give it and He multiplies back to me by His power."

If it is of grace, faith must be involved.

Romans 4:16:
> **"Therefore it is of faith that it might be according to grace, so that the promise might be sure to all the seed, not only to those who are of the law, but also to those who are of the faith of Abraham, who is the father of us all."**

What is the promise attached to the tithe?

Malachi 3:10:
> **"'Bring all the tithes into the storehouse,
> That there may be food in My house,
> And try Me now in this,'
> Says the Lord of hosts,
> 'If I will not open for you the windows of heaven
> And pour out for you such blessing
> That there will not be room enough to receive it.'"**

The promise is that God will pour out a blessing of abundance until there is no room to receive it. The Bible says: " ... it is of faith that it might be according to grace, so that the promise might be sure to all the seed ..." (Rom 4:16).

Grace guarantees the blessing of the tithe to all when we begin to appropriate it by faith.

This is why tithing has not worked for many because they do it with a legalistic attitude of the law and the law always works condemnation, reinforces the sense of guilt and shuts down your faith.

Romans 3:19:

"Now we know that whatever the law says, it says to those who are under the law, that every mouth may be stopped, and all the world may become guilty before God."

The law will cause your mouth to be stopped where you cannot make a confession of faith and appropriate the blessings of tithing because you are filled with a consciousness of guilt and shame.

With Jesus as the High Priest of the new covenant you have a voice before God, and you can boldly appropriate the blessings of tithing.

You can declare confidently in faith: "I have given my tithes, and the floodgates of heaven's blessings are open unto me. God's superabundant prosperity is manifesting in my life and there is no lack in Jesus' Name."

15

JESUS CHRIST, MELCHIZEDEK AND THE TITHE

Hebrews 6.19-20; 7:1-3:
"This hope we have as an anchor of the soul, both sure and steadfast, and which enters the Presence behind the veil, where the forerunner has entered for us, even Jesus, having become High Priest forever according to the order of Melchizedek.
"For this Melchizedek, king of Salem, priest of the Most High God, who met Abraham returning from the slaughter of the kings and blessed him, to whom also Abraham gave a tenth part of all, first being translated "king of righteousness," and then also king of Salem, meaning "king of peace," without father, without mother, without genealogy, having neither beginning of days nor end of life, but made like the Son of God, remains a priest continually."

The first mention of the tithe in the new covenant is taken directly from its first mention under the Old Testament from the story of Abraham's encounter with this mysterious figure Melchizedek.

Our understanding of the place of the tithe in the new covenant must involve the study of Melchizedek.

The inspired writer of the book of Hebrews quotes Psalm 110:4 in referring to the New Testament Priesthood of Jesus as a priesthood after the order of Melchisedek.

> "The Lord has sworn
> And will not relent,
> 'You are a priest forever
> According to the order of Melchizedek.'"

The Hebrew word translated as "order" also means "manner" or "mode". Jesus is declared to be priest in the same manner and mode as Melchizedek.

The Greek word used in translating this word is " taxis" from the word "tasso" which means to arrange in order, to set in order, arrangement, disposition especially of troops, an order or rank in state or society. We get the word "'taxonomy'" from this word. Taxonomy in the life sciences is the science of classification. You can take animals in the class of lions and when you have seen one lion you have a picture of how other lions function. Jesus Christ is a Priest in the order of Melchizedek.

That means the priestly duties of Melchizedek as revealed in the Scriptures give us an insight to the Priestly ministry of Jesus Christ today. If Melchizedek received tithes from Abraham that points to the fact that Jesus Christ, High Priest of the new covenant receives tithes from His people today under the new covenant. This fact is an act of grace from God to us human beings through Jesus Christ.

Jesus Christ receiving your tithes today is an act of grace coming from the throne of God to you today. Let this fact be etched into our consciousness.

Hebrews 7:1-3:

"For this Melchizedek, king of Salem, priest of the Most High God, who met Abraham returning from the slaughter of the kings and blessed him, to whom also Abraham gave a tenth part of all, first being translated 'king of righteousness', and then also king of Salem, meaning 'king of peace', without father, without mother, without genealogy, having neither beginning of days nor end of life, but made like the Son of

God, remains a priest continually."

The Bible does not tell us that Melchizedek was the pre-incarnate Christ because the words "pre-incarnate" means before He took on flesh and blood. That means Christ before the incarnation. That would make Melchizedek a spirit personality. That cannot be true because the Bible says: " He was king of a city called Salem", which is said to be present day Jerusalem. Melchizedek was a human being who ruled over a city called Salem and he was a king over that city and Melchizedek was not his personal name, but this was his title as the ruler of Salem at that time just as the rulers of Egypt were referred to as pharaoh and the kings of the Philistines were called Abimelech.

The Scriptures, however, deliberately leave blank the exact identity of this personality and does not give us his genealogy in order to create a picture of the coming priesthood of Jesus Christ. This is the point the writer of the Book of Hebrew is communicating.

It says: " He is without Father, without Mother, without genealogy, having neither beginning of days nor end of life."

This means, according to the records of Scriptures, we have no idea of who his father was or who his mother was or what his earthly genealogy was. We have no idea when he was born or when he died. There is an inspired silence about these aspects of the life of this personality to create a resemblance of the coming eternal priesthood of Jesus Christ.

THE PICTURE OF A COMING PRIESTHOOD

Hebrews 7:3:
" ... without father, without mother, without genealogy, having neither beginning of days nor end of life, but made like the Son of God, remains a priest continually."

The writer of the book of Hebrews tells us that Scriptures in not giving us records of Melchizedek's ancestry, or when his life began or ended: " Melchizedek was made like unto the Son of God."

The Greek word used here "aphomoioo" is used only in this instance in the New Testament. It means "to make like" or "liken or make very much like". The word means to produce a facsimile or a copy.

When you see the facsimile or copy of a document, they look alike but the original is what authenticates the copy. Melchizedek, so to speak, can be likened to a copy or a fax of Jesus Christ from the future. Jesus Christ is the authenticating original of which Melchizedek was a facsimile copy. In business transactions today copies are accepted in lieu of original only as long as the original can be produced on demand.

Melchizedek could only collect tithes from Abraham because Jesus Christ collects tithes today. This is the basis of the argument of the writer of the book of Hebrews to demonstrate the superiority of the priesthood of Jesus Christ and the abrogation of the Levitical Priesthood.

The Aramaic translation of Hebrews 7:3 uses the word "demutha" which means a form, an image or a pattern and a type. In other words, in Melchizedek, Scriptures are giving to us a form, a pattern, a type, an image, or a picture of the coming eternal priesthood of Jesus Christ.

That is the relationship of Melchizedek to Jesus Christ. In the ministry of Melchizedek, Scriptures were just simulating the coming priesthood of Jesus Christ. Hence what we see Melchizedek doing at that point in time is a pointer to what Jesus Christ does today in His role as High Priest of the church.

It is very obvious by looking at the ministry of Melchizedek that we can infer without a doubt that Jesus Christ receives tithes in His capacity as High Priest of the new covenant. He receives these however not directly but through His appointed and authorised representatives in the earth.

"In Scriptures all lines of thought and history, of type and prophecy, converge and meet in one point, the Messiah. Christ is set forth in the words, deeds and persons of prophets, priests and kings." (Adolph Saphir)

Melchizedek received tithes only because Jesus Christ as High Priest of the new Covenant receives tithes from His people today.

16

THE STATEMENTS OF JESUS CHRIST ABOUT THE TITHE

Looking at the account of the gospels we see that Jesus Christ talked very little on the tithe. When we examine His teachings on financial matters, He practically did not mention the issue of the tithe. However, Jesus Christ' relative silence on the tithe can be understood now in the light of the rule or canon of first mention in Biblical interpretation.

It was a deliberate and inspired silence because the Levitical Priesthood and the temple in which they carried out their work in the days of Jesus Christ's ministry was about to come to an end, to be replaced with a new priesthood and a new temple.

His silence, however, did not mean that the principle of the tithe would be done away with. As we have seen practices may differ, but principles don't change. Principles are timeless by their very nature.

THE TITHE IN PERSPECTIVE

Matthew 23:23:
"Woe to you, scribes and Pharisees, hypocrites! For you pay tithe of mint and anise and cummin, and have neglected the weightier matters of the law: justice and mercy and faith. These you ought to have done, without leaving the others undone."

The Pharisees and scribes were very meticulous about the details of the law and took this into the practice of tithing. They tithed practically everything.

The mint plant was a herbal plant that had a clean and aromatic smell. It was used as strewing plants at home and in the temple and was also one of the bitter herbs of the pascal feast. The Greek word for it was "heduosmon" literarily meaning "having a sweet smell". It was also a medicinal herb.

Then the dill or the anise was a seasoning plant which also had carminative properties. It was a pot garden plant, and the Romans chewed it to keep up an agreeable moisture in their mouths and to sweeten their breath, a habit which some Orientals still have today for the same reason.

The Pharisees were so scrupulous about tithing that the Talmud speaks of the donkey of a certain rabbi which was so well trained as to refuse corn from which tithes had not been taken!

Jesus Christ, however, did not criticize them for their tithing practices. He chastised them for their religious hypocrisy and legalistic attitude.

They had become so religious and legalistic to the point of leaving out God's intention for giving the law.

True, God incorporated the tithe into the law of Moses under the old covenant, but it was not in a spirit of bringing condemnation and guilt on the people, but in a spirit of grace.

God wanted to help His people in their finances. The Pharisees had lost sight of this fact.

Jesus calls their attention back to God's intention for giving the law. He refers to it as the weightier matters of the law. We can refer to it as of the original intent of the law.

In the United States the doctrine of original intent is prevalent in interpreting the constitution. The original framers of the constitution are not alive to explain what they meant when they wrote the constitution. Therefore, lawyers and judges refer to the concept of "original intent". In other words, what was uppermost in the minds of the framers when they wrote the constitution, what is it that they were trying to achieve? What was the goal that they sought to accomplish. The belief is that if the interpretation of the constitution is guided by the concept of original intent, judges will aways give rulings that will produce outcomes consistent with what the founders of the constitution had in mind.

The Pharisees and scribes were scrupulous about tithing but were missing out on God's original intent for giving the law because of their religious and legalistic mindset. Jesus said to them "woe unto you"! They were not getting the results God had in mind for tithing.

In the same way, if you leave the grace of God out of tithing, it becomes a mere legalistic and religious exercise, and you could miss out on the blessings of God. This, I believe, is the reason why tithing today has become a very contentions subject in the body of Christ. Jesus hit the nail on the head in His brief commentary on the tithing of the Pharisees and scribes.

To get into some more detail about this concept of God's intent for giving the law, let us look at Matthew 23:23 from the Hebrew Gospel of Matthew by George Howard.

"Woe to them the sages and Pharisees who tithe (mint), dill and pomegranate but who commit robbery (and leave undone) that which is weightier, that is the judgements of the Torah which are: kindness, truth, and faithfulness. These are commands worthy of doing; one should not forget them."

The Hebrew word translated as "weightier" is the same word translated as "glory" which is "kabod" and that word means "that which is weighty, serious and important".

We can therefore refer to the weightier matters of the law as those matters that were weighty, serious, and heavy on God's mind in giving the law. In other words, what was uppermost on God's mind when He gave the law.

In looking at the attitude of the Pharisees and scribes you would think the tithe was what was most important, heavy, and serious on God's mind when He gave the law. This is why Jesus chastised them. He was not criticising their tithing practices, but He was correcting their thinking, to bring them in line with what was most important to God in giving the law.

Jesus reveals what was most important, heavy, serious and uppermost in God's mind for giving the law as "righteousness, mercy, and truth".

The Lord Jesus revealed the original intention for the law here. It was "righteousness, mercy, and truth". Now that is huge!

Punishment is not what God had in mind when He gave the law. He had grace in mind. He was really after meeting the needs of people. He had mercy in mind. The only way they could receive His grace and mercy was to recognise that in their sinful condition they could not merit the blessings of God. The law reveals man's sinfulness and guiltiness so that he could cry out to God for His mercy and grace. The Pharisees and scribes were tithing scrupulously to earn merit points with God.

> **Jeremiah 9:23-24:**
> **"Thus says the Lord:**
> **'Let not the wise man glory in his wisdom,**
> **Let not the mighty man glory in his might,**
> **Nor let the rich man glory in his riches;**
> **But let him who glories glory in this,**
> **That he understands and knows Me,**
> **That I am the Lord, exercising**
> **lovingkindness, judgment, and**
> **righteousness in the earth.**
> **For in these I delight,' says the Lord."**

This Scripture tells us that greater than human wisdom, greater than wealth and power is "understanding and knowing God" and the key to knowing God is "lovingkindness", which is the same as mercy, judgement, and righteousness.

The Pharisees and scribes were the religious experts of the day. They were scrupulous about tithing, but they did not know God.

Jesus is putting the tithe in its proper context. He is telling them to give their tithes for the same reason why God placed in it the law and that is for righteousness, lovingkindness and truth.

God wants to show people His forgiveness, mercy, and grace in all areas of life including their finances. If your financial situation is messed up, you can look to God through Jesus Christ for His forgiveness and believe His mercy and grace will turn your situation around.

Hebrews 4:16:

"Let us therefore come boldly to the throne of grace, that we may obtain mercy and find grace to help in time of need."

God placed the laws concerning tithing there so that the needs of people can be ministered to in truth, righteousness, and mercy.

There are so called ministers of the gospel who today are using legalism and religious manipulation to collect tithes from people but not really ministering to their needs in any meaningful way. The people are still bound in ignorance and religion. That is a form of robbery and all that will change as the truth of God's word comes alive in these last days.

You can religiously manipulate people and collect tithes from them all you want but if you cancel or leave off righteousness, mercy and truth then people's need will be left unmet. It is this kind of religious manipulation that Jesus Christ spoke against.

The Pharisees and the scribes in their scrupulousness toward the tithe and other lesser matters of the law had left off the major matter or what can be referred to as the real intention of God for giving the law.

GOD IS NOT AFTER YOUR MONEY

Jesus Christ castigated the Pharisees and scribes because they took advantage of the people's ignorance and used religion to manipulate them and in doing so kept them under their selfish control. Religious people do the same thing today.

Unlike God, many so-called preachers and ministers of the gospel use religion to manipulate money from the pockets of the very people whom they are supposed to be helping with the gospel message.

> **2 Corinthians 2:17**
> **(Classic Amplified Translation):**
> "For we are not, as so many, (like hucksters making a trade of) peddling the word of God (short-changing and adulterating the divine message); but as (men) of sincerity (and the purest motive), but as (commissioned and sent) from God, we speak (His message in Christ the Messiah) in the (very) sight (and presence) of God in Christ."

This is what many have done with the word of God. They have adulterated it by making it say what it was never intended to say to manipulate people into giving them their money.

However, God's attitude is the exact opposite. He is not after anybody's money. The Bible says the earth is the Lord's and the fullness thereof. He owns it all.

> **Psalm 50:7-15:**
> "Hear, O My people, and I will speak,
> O Israel, and I will testify against you;
> I am God, your God!
> I will not rebuke you for your sacrifices
> Or your burnt offerings,
> Which are continually before Me.
> I will not take a bull from your house,
> Nor goats out of your folds.
> For every beast of the forest is Mine,
> And the cattle on a thousand hills.
> I know all the birds of the mountains,
> And the wild beasts of the field are Mine.
> If I were hungry, I would not tell you;
> For the world is Mine, and all its fullness."

God told the people: "If I were hungry, I would not tell you for the earth is the Lord's and the fullness thereof." He does not need anybody's permission to get in here and take any of it if He needed it. He owns it all because He created it all.

However, God is love and His method of taking care of our needs enables us to grow in partaking of His divine nature which is love. God wants to meet your needs but in meeting your needs He gets you involved in helping other people to get their own needs met. This is the reason for God's principles regarding tithing and giving.

TITHING WILL NOT SAVE YOU

In the gospels there are three places where Jesus Christ mentioned the tithe. The first one is Matthew 23:23 which we have seen above. The second one is Luke 11:42 which is really a restatement by Luke of Jesus' statement in Matthew 23:23. Then the third one is Jesus's mention of it in a parable.

> **Luke 18:9-14:**
> **"Also He spoke this parable to some who trusted in themselves that they were righteous, and despised others: 'Two men went up to the temple to pray, one a Pharisee and the other a tax collector. The Pharisee stood and prayed thus with himself, 'God, I thank You that I am not like other men—extortioners, unjust, adulterers, or even as this tax collector. I fast twice a week; I give tithes of all that I possess.' And the tax collector, standing afar off, would not so much as raise his eyes to heaven, but beat his breast, saying, 'God, be merciful to me a sinner!' 'I tell you, this man went down to his house justified rather than the other; for everyone who exalts himself will be humbled, and he who humbles himself will be exalted.'"**

One of the most extreme statements I have heard concerning the tithe was when in a church service I heard the pastor, in an attempt to collect tithes and offerings from the congregation, say to them: "If you don't pay your tithes, you are going to hell." I have since then heard this same statement from other ministers of the gospel.

Is it correct to say that believers who have trusted in Jesus Christ for their salvation can go to hell because they are not tithing? Going to heaven or hell is a matter of eternal salvation and should be taken with the utmost caution and seriousness.

By examining the parable of Jesus in the verses above we can get an answer to this question. Luke tells us that Jesus gave this parable to "some who trusted in themselves that they were righteous and despised others". In other words, they trusted their works to merit them justification before God. They had been deceived into thinking that they had good standing before God because they kept the requirements of the law better than anyone else.

The Bible however tells us that all the righteousness of our keeping the law is like filthy rags before God (Is 64:6).

The Pharisees boasted in the fact that they kept God's laws better than anyone else, but the Bible says to break just one of the ten commandments is as good as breaking them all.

James 2:10:
"For whoever shall keep the whole law, and yet stumble in one point, he is guilty of all."

Jesus taught that breaking the law in our thoughts is just as bad as breaking it in our actions.

In the parable of Jesus, the Pharisee went to the temple and prayed, quoting his own works, which included the works of giving tithes on everything as the reason why God should justify him. In other words, he thought he could be saved based on his works.

The Bible says: "… the Pharisee stood and prayed thus with himself …" The Greek translation says: " He stood and prayed to himself…" In other words, he was his own god. He was trusting in his own ability, his own works to justify and therefore save him before God.

Whether a person goes to heaven or hell is a matter of salvation. According to the New Testament salvation is based on justification of righteousness.

Romans 10:4-13 gives us God's salvation plan for all people, and it says nothing about tithing:

> **"For Christ is the end of the law for righteousness to everyone who believes.**

"For Moses writes about the righteousness which is of the law, 'The man who does those things shall live by them.' But the righteousness of faith speaks in this way, 'Do not say in your heart, Who will ascend into heaven?' (that is, to bring Christ down from above) or 'Who will descend into the abyss?' (that is, to bring Christ up from the dead). But what does it say? 'The word is near you, in your mouth and in your heart' (that is, the word of faith which we preach): that if you confess with your mouth the Lord Jesus and believe in your heart that God has raised Him from the dead, you will be saved. For with the heart one believes unto righteousness, and with the mouth confession is made unto salvation. For the Scripture says, 'Whoever believes on Him will not be put to shame.' For there is no distinction between Jew and Greek, for the same Lord over all is rich to all who call upon Him. For 'whoever calls on the name of the Lord shall be saved.'"

Jesus Christ is the end of law for righteousness or justification. The Pharisee was depending on himself and his works to earn him justification and therefore salvation before God.

He was hoping to make it to heaven on his own power and merit and he quoted his excellent tithing records as one of the reasons why he would make it to heaven and escape going to hell.

The Bible says: "He prayed to himself". He thought he was praying to God but in reality, he was praying to himself. He was trusting in himself.

People who teach and preach today that a person will not make it to heaven because they are not tithing are no different from this religious Pharisee.

In Romans 10:4-13 we see God's Road map of salvation and getting us to heaven. Tithing is not mentioned there. It is based on the merit of Jesus Christ and His work at calvary and in the fact that He was raised from the dead for our justification.

The tax collector on the other hand received God's justification or we could say: "He was saved by God because he did not trust in works but called on God to make atonement for his sins." It is very interesting that the Bible says: " … he stood afar off".

This was a reflection of the attitude of the Jewish society towards tax collectors. They were regarded as the worst among sinners and the Pharisees and other religious leaders of the day taught that tax collectors could not be saved. They regarded their case as hopeless and every Sabbath day the synagogue official read out the list of tax collectors and told the congregation to have nothing to do with them and that they could not be saved.

The tax collector standing far from the temple prayed to God: " … be merciful to me a sinner!"

This is referring to the Jewish day of atonement. On that day the high priest took the blood of a goat into the holy of holies and there made an atonement for the sins of Israel. However, the common teaching of that day was that this atonement did not include the tax collectors. Hence Jesus said, "he stood afar off from temple and said to God 'atone for me'".

He was calling on God to do for him what the blood of bulls and goats could not do for him according to the Pharisees of his day. He was calling on God Himself to be his High Priest and make atonement for him. This is what Jesus Christ did for us. In Jesus Christ, God took on flesh and blood and did for us all that the blood of bulls and goats could not do under the old covenant.

Hebrews 9:28:

"… so Christ was offered once to bear the sins of many. To those who eagerly wait for Him He will appear a second time, apart from sin, for salvation."

God in Christ Jesus has done for us all that the blood of bulls and goats could not do under the old covenant.

He is able to cleanse us from all our sins with the precious blood of Jesus and that is the basis of our faith for salvation, not our record of tithing.

When we face God on the day of judgement it is not our tithing records that will decide whether we go to heaven or hell. What God will look at is whether we trusted Jesus Christ for our salvation.

The Pharisee trusted in himself, his works and excellent tithing records but remained condemned and guilty before God. The tax collector, regarded as the worst among sinners, trusted in God's atonement for his sins and went way justified and saved before God.

Do not tithe like the religious hypocrites of the days of Jesus Christ or even today to make it to heaven. Only Jesus and His sacrifice at calvary can get you to heaven. When you tithe do it in faith and for the right reasons out of a heart of gratefulness and love for God and because you want others through your giving to experience God's grace and mercy as you have also experienced it. Then God will step in and multiply it back to you and you will see your financial needs being met according to God's riches in glory.

If you are in a situation currently that is so bad that you are unable to tithe, don't let the devil put you under condemnation with religious teachings and indoctrination. Give what you can and trust God to turn your situation around and put you back where you can begin to tithe consistently.

17

GOD'S FINANCIAL PLAN FOR THE GOSPEL

In discussing the tithe and examining if it is for the believer living under the New Testament, we shall be looking into God's plan to finance the gospel and the believer's role in this plan.

The responsibility to take the gospel to the whole world was placed on the entire church, which is the worldwide community of believers under Jesus Christ as Head.

Matthew 28:18-20:

"And Jesus came and spoke to them, saying, 'All authority has been given to Me in heaven and on earth. Go therefore and make disciples of all the nations, baptizing them in the name of the Father and of the Son and of the Holy Spirit, teaching them to observe all things that I have commanded you; and lo, I am with you always, even to the end of the age.'"

Jesus said "… go into all the world, preach the gospel and make disciples …" This commission will require the use of money because money is the medium by which goods and services are exchanged in this world.

Ecclesiastes 10:19:
"A feast is made for laughter,
And wine makes merry;
But money answers everything."

If this be the case God must have a financial plan by which the great commission can be carried out successfully by the church.

It is not consistent with God's character to have Him give us an assignment without a plan by which to carry it out. God's financial plan to carry out the great commission must be laid out in Scripture. It is up to us in the church to find out what God's financial plan is with the help of the Holy Spirit whom He has sent to guide us into all truth.

2 Chronicles 31:2-4:

"And Hezekiah appointed the divisions of the priests and the Levites according to their divisions, each man according to his service, the priests and Levites for burnt offerings and peace offerings, to serve, to give thanks, and to praise in the gates of the camp of the Lord. The king also appointed a portion of his possessions for the burnt offerings: for the morning and evening burnt offerings, the burnt offerings for the Sabbaths and the New Moons and the set feasts, as it is written in the Law of the Lord.

"Moreover he commanded the people who dwelt in Jerusalem to contribute support for the priests and the Levites, that they might devote themselves to the Law of the Lord."

Hezekiah was one of Israel's greatest kings ever. He had great insight into the cardinal place temple worship and the priesthood held in the nation. With that understanding he proceeded to restore temple worship and give the priesthood its place and honour in the life of the nation. His reforms went on to produce a national revival of worship in the land as God honoured them, prospering his reign and the land of Israel.

Hezekiah's reforms all stemmed out of God's instructions to Israel through Moses, which were then documented and given to them as the Torah or God's written instructions. It says Hezekiah commanded the people to contribute support for the priests and Levites so that they could devote themselves to the Law of the Lord.

The Hebrew word "devote" does not mean just to be strong and firm, but it also means to be fixed or established in a particular place. The work of the priesthood was so central and important to the needs of the people that God instructed that the priests give themselves totally to that office and not engage in anything else. Hezekiah realised that the salvation of the nation depended on this priestly ministry.

In other to ensure this, Hezekiah commanded people in line with God's written word to contribute support for the priests and Levites. This contributed support would take care of their livelihood, and that would be the source of their income as they rendered this vital service to God's covenant people. The Hebrew word translated as "support" is "manah" and this word means to count, to enumerate, to weigh out, to officially designate an allotted or allocated portion, and it also means a portion due.

Hezekiah realised from the written word of God that a certain portion of the income of the Israelites had been officially designated by God, the Head of the nation for the priesthood.

Hezekiah understood God's financial plan as God outlined it in the Old Testament.

The people followed God's instructions as Hezekiah issued it forth to the nation and the result was tremendous blessing on the land.

2 Chronicles 31:5:
"As soon as the commandment was circulated, the children of Israel brought in abundance the firstfruits of grain and wine, oil and honey, and of all the produce of the field; and they brought in abundantly the tithe of everything."

In verse four the commandment was to bring forth the allotted or designated portion to the priests and Levites and verse five tells us how the people understood the word "manah" or allotted, or officially designated or measured out portion. They understood it to be firstfruits and tithes.

When the people got in line with God's financial plan they prospered.

> **2 Chronicles 31:20-21:**
> **"Thus Hezekiah did throughout all Judah, and he did what was good and right and true before the Lord his God. And in every work that he began in the service of the house of God, in the law and in the commandment, to seek his God, he did it with all his heart. So he prospered."**

It is worth noting here that Hezekiah as king of the nation did not invent any special programme to address poverty in the land. He simply took God's prosperity plan as outlined in the Bible and implemented it in the land and the result was that whole nation prospered from following God's plan.

How does this apply to God's financial plan for the gospel in the new Covenant?

> **1 Corinthians 9:13-14:**
> **"Do you not know that those who minister the holy things eat of the things of the temple, and those who serve at the altar partake of the offerings of the altar? Even so the Lord has commanded that those who preach the gospel should live from the gospel."**

Who are those who ministered holy things in the Old Testament? It was the priests and the Levites. Who are those who served at the altar under the Old Testament? It was the priests and Levites. How were their needs taken care of? What was the source of their income? From the Scripture above we see that it was the tithes and offerings of the people. That was officially designated as their allotted portion or due, in other words, to carry out the work of the priesthood and minister to the needs of the people.

The Scripture above states that "even so the Lord has directed". Who is the Lord being referred to here? It is Jesus Christ, the Head of the Church, giving direction to the church and outlining His financial plan for the gospel. This plan is taken directly from His plan under the old covenant. It says: " ... even so the Lord has commanded that those who preach the gospel should live from the gospel". How are they to live from the gospel? We have the answer. It is the same way the priests and Levites got their income under the Old Testament. It was based on the tithes and offerings of the people.

We see then the Lord bringing the same principle of tithes and offerings from the Old Testament into the New Testament. It is the same plan based on God's timeless and unchanging principles of financial success. When Israel followed God's plan under the old covenant they prospered and if we do the same in the New Testament we shall also prosper.

18

BLESSING PARTNERSHIP OF TITHING

Now that we have seen that God's financial model for the priesthood based on the tithes and offerings of God's people has been imported into the New Testament let us look in some more details into the great tithing Scripture of the Bible.

Malachi 3:10:
"'Bring all the tithes into the storehouse,
That there may be food in My house,
And try Me now in this,'
Says the Lord of hosts,
'If I will not open for you the windows of heaven
And pour out for you such blessing
That there will not be room enough to receive it.'"

God is the one who makes the provision, but He speaks to His people to bring all the tithes into the storehouse that there might be meat or provision in His house. God could unilaterally on His own decide to rain down resources from heaven for the work of the ministry, but He has chosen not to do it that way. He wants to go into partnership with us to provide for the work of the ministry. He wants to work with us in partnership to make finances available for the work of gospel ministry.

God does not force this partnership on any of us but wants us to willingly accept His offer of partnership and that makes Him involved in causing the finances to come.

It is not only going toward the meeting of our needs but through our tithing He is able to get the gospel out to those who need it in the world.

God's supernatural power or grace becomes involved in our finances to cause our needs to be supernaturally met.

God was offering to go into a financial partnership of blessing with the people. That principle remains until now because principles are timeless.

In his letter to the Philippians, Paul illustrates this same principle of partnership with God in financial matters. The Philippian believers had become Paul's partners and more than once they sent resources to enable him to carry on with his ministry. Because of this partnership Paul declared that their needs would be supernaturally met by God.

Philippians 4:19
"And my God shall supply all your need according to His riches in glory by Christ Jesus."

In other words, as they operated by the principle of partnership with God in their finances God would intervene on their behalf to cause their needs to be supernaturally met according to His riches in glory.

In tithing we get into blessing partnership with God where our needs are supernaturally met through His power, and He works in us and through us to provide finances to get the gospel of blessing to others who need it.

THE DEVOURER REBUKED

God gives his people a promise that is peculiar to tithing only. He promised them that if they would come into the blessing partnership with Him through tithing, He would rebuke the devourer for their sakes.

Malachi 3:11:
"'And I will rebuke the devourer for your sakes,
So that he will not destroy the fruit of your ground,
Nor shall the vine fail to bear fruit for you in the field,'
Says the Lord of hosts."

Tithing is a covenant partnership that gives God legal grounds to rebuke the devourer from bringing financial destruction on you. He has a stake in your finances as much as you and that gives Him grounds to move against Satan the destroyer on your behalf.

The literal Hebrew translation says: "I will rebuke the devourer to you." In other words, you get the benefit of Him rebuking the devourer. God is not the one who needs to have the devourer rebuked because heaven is His domain, and the devil cannot get in there and destroy anything. He was kicked out of heaven a long time ago. It is people on earth that need the devourer rebuked and God promised that if we would get into the tithing partnership of blessing with Him then He would move on our behalf and rebuke the devourer. We have the covenant right to claim this promise from God as tithers.

19

AM I CURSED FOR NOT TITHING?

Now let us examine one more statement that makes many people think that Malachi 3:6-12 is not referring to the New Testament believer.

Malachi 3:9:
"You are cursed with a curse,
For you have robbed Me,
Even this whole nation."

They say this verse speaks of the people being cursed because they haven't tithed and then they proceed to quote Galatians 3:13-14:

"Christ has redeemed us from the curse of the law, having become a curse for us (for it is written, 'Cursed is everyone who hangs on a tree'), that the blessing of Abraham might come upon the Gentiles in Christ Jesus, that we might receive the promise of the Spirit through faith."

They argue that Jesus Christ has redeemed us from the curse in His redemptive work at the cross and so it would be unscriptural to speak of a believer under the New Testament as being cursed.

Yes, it is true that legally speaking Christ has redeemed us from the curse of the law listed in Deuteronomy 28:15-68.

The curse of the law can be broadly summarised as spiritual death, poverty, sickness and disease. Jesus Christ in His death, burial and resurrection has redeemed us from it. However, we must walk in the reality of redemption through living by the word of God.

Galatians 5:1:
"Stand fast therefore in the liberty by which Christ has made us free, and do not be entangled again with a yoke of bondage."

How then can Malachi 3:9 apply to the believer today?

First taking a look at this Scripture in the Companion Bible, we see some interesting notes on it.

The Companion Bible commenting on Malachi 3:9 says: " ... the primitive Hebrew text of this verse says 'ye have cursed me with a curse.' This was the original way it was documented. God was telling the people they had cursed Him with a curse."

The Sopherim were the scribes that meticulously copied and reproduced Old Testament texts. They were highly professional and dedicated in their work of copying the written word of God exactly as it was transmitted.

However, there were 18 instances in the Old Testament where they did not translate exactly what they saw in the original copy because they thought to do so literally would amount to irreverence to God. In these instances, they attached special notes calling people's attention to what they had done and the reason they translated it the way they did. These are called the 18 emendations of the Sopherim, and the Companion Bible lists these 18 emendations in appendix 33 attached within it. Malachi 3:9 is one of those 18 emendations. The primitive text said: " You have cursed Me with a curse."

In other words, God was not saying primarily that the people were cursed but that they had cursed Him in not bringing their tithes. The Sopherim thought to translate this verbatim would amount to irreverence to God and so they translated it in a way they thought would be reverential to God by saying "you are cursed with a curse for you have robbed Me even this whole nation."

However, God did not mean to do any irreverence to Himself when He told the people that "they were cursing Him by not bringing their tithes".

A closer look at the word "curse" used in this verse will give more insight into what God was saying to His people. The Hebrew word translated as curse here is "arar" and this word primarily means to "isolate".

This is what God was saying to them: "You have isolated Me from your finances by not bringing in your tithes."

That means the people had cut Him off from being involved in their finances and by so doing He could not move on their behalf. This is the "curse" God was referring to.

God had offered them a financial partnership of blessing whereby He would be involved in their finances and take care of their financial needs and through that partnership keep the devourer out of their finances. Because they had broken that partnership God was consequently on the outside of their finances. By cutting God out of their finances they had by default opened the door wide for the enemy to inflict financial harm on them. In essence God was not cursing them, they were cursing themselves by isolating God from their finances.

Can the believer do that today? Absolutely yes! Christ has redeemed us from the curse of the law but if we get into disobedience, we can cut God off our finances and that will allow the enemy in to cause all kinds of financial problems for us.

God was revealing to the people the source of their problems and it is the same today because God has not changed, and the devil also has not changed. God was showing them how they could cooperate with Him to resolve their situation, and that is how we too can cooperate with God to resolve our financial issues.

When it comes to finances God does not want us to do it all alone. He wants to come into partnership with us so that he can act on our behalf. This is God's offer of His grace to us in our financial affairs.

As we examine these Scriptures more closely, we can see that God was speaking to Israel through the prophet Malachi, but the timeless principles contained therein also apply to us today in the New Testament.

Malachi 3:9 in the concordant version of the Old Testament confirms the commentaries in the Companion Bible along these lines. It read as follows:

> " ... with a curse you curse Me and Me you are defrauding – the whole nation of it."

The word translated as "defraud" here in the King James version is the word translated as "rob".

The Hebrew word translated as rob is " qabay" and the word also means to limit and fix. That ties in with the Hebrew word "to curse" which means to "'isolate'". When you isolate someone, you place boundaries and limits around them beyond which they cannot move. In other words, you have the person fixed in a particular place. God said His people had done that to Him in their finances. He wanted to do more for them and through them, but they were not cooperating with Him.

Disobedience to God's financial principle outlined to us in His word can certainly place us in the situation where God cannot do more through us and with us.

NEITHER GIVE PLACE TO THE DEVIL

God told the people through the prophet Malachi that they had robbed Him. We can however see this in a larger context that they were robbing or denying Him His place in their lives the opportunity to bless them. In doing that they were cursing themselves. They were inflicting harm on themselves.

The question to ask should not be whether we are cursed if we don't tithe. God is showing us that something bigger is at stake here. The fact is that we are cutting God off our finances by not following God's instructions to us regarding our finances. Through disobedience to God's instructions, we give place to the enemy to cause us harm financially.

John 10:10:
"The thief does not come except to steal, and to kill, and to

destroy. I have come that they may have life, and that they may have it more abundantly."

Satan is the thief and the robber, and his ultimate purpose is to steal from God the opportunity to bless us and bless others through us. The area of finances is one area Satan certainly can work to block what God is doing through the gospel to transform lives.

Ephesians 4:27: (New English Bible)
"Leave no loophole for the devil."

By not carrying out God's instructions we leave a loophole for the devil which he can exploit to cause us a lot of damage and certainly in our finances. This is what God's people had done under the old covenant and we certainly can learn from that and be wiser in our relationship with God.

2 Timothy 3:16-17:
"All Scripture is given by inspiration of God, and is profitable for doctrine, for reproof, for correction, for instruction in righteousness, that the man of God may be complete, thoroughly equipped for every good work."

All Scripture includes Malachi 3:6-12 and God had it written down for us and when it is rightly divided, we can profit from it as we gain a correct understanding of it. We are not to come out condemned and guilty, but we get to see where we may be missing it and then we can start walking in the light.

20

GRACE REMOVES THE PRESSURE

One of the reasons why the subject of tithing has become so controversial today is that unfortunately many so-called ministers of the gospel and pastors have quoted Scriptures completely out of context to put pressure on people and manipulate them religiously, to get them to give the tithe.

When you hear a statement like "if you don't tithe you are robbing God and you are going to hell!" that puts you under tremendous pressure because no child of God in his rightful mind will want to do anything that will put them in danger of going to hell.

As far as I am concerned, that kind of statement is worse than placing a gun to someone's head and saying to them: "Your money or your life". The reason I say that is very simple. Which one is more consequential in your mind as a child of God: dying physically and going to heaven or dying and going to hell? Telling someone: "If you don't tithe you are going to hell," is a far greater threat than putting a gun to their head demanding their money.

This is the reason why there is so much controversy about tithing. It is because the clergy have used religious manipulation to place pressure on people to give their money, and people naturally rebel when you put them under pressure. They start to seek a way out of that pressure. When you tell people "You are cursed when you don't tithe", it is pressure. When you preach to people and tell them God won't bless them when they don't tithe and that they are robbing God when they don't tithe, then you are putting them under pressure that comes with guilty conscience.

> **Ephesians 1:3:**
> **"Blessed be the God and Father of our Lord Jesus Christ, who has blessed us with every spiritual blessing in the heavenly places in Christ."**

In Christ Jesus God has already blessed us and we cannot do anything to merit the blessings of God. All we can do now is appropriate what God has already made available to us in Christ Jesus.

> **Philippians 4:15-17:**
> **"Now you Philippians know also that in the beginning of the gospel, when I departed from Macedonia, no church shared with me concerning giving and receiving but you only. For even in Thessalonica you sent aid once and again for my necessities. Not that I seek the gift, but I seek the fruit that abounds to your account."**

We see the apostle Paul teach here that when he started out taking the gospel to the gentiles no church communicated with him concerning giving and receiving. The Greek word translated as "communicated" means partnership.

These churches with their gentile background knew nothing about giving and receiving. They knew nothing about tithing. Paul and the rest of the apostles were silent on tithing and as we have seen in previous sections of this book this silence on the tithing was an inspired silence because the revelation of the New Testament priesthood of Jesus Christ had not yet come.

We don't however see the apostle Paul telling them they were cursed and that they were robbing God and that they were going to hell because they were not tithing. He did not use any such language on the churches because that would be completely out of line with God's word and would have amounted to religious manipulation. Rather we see Paul saying to them " blessed be God who has blessed us with all spiritual blessings in heavenly places in Christ Jesus." Paul or Peter did not tell them they were cursed but kept bringing them the revelation knowledge of God's word so that they could understand God's financial plan.

When Paul taught the people about finances his attitude was " not that I seek the gift, but I seek the fruit abounding to your account." He taught the people God's financial plan which includes giving but he was not after their money. He wanted to see their financial needs met. He wanted them to experience the joy of being part of God's blessing plan to the world with the gospel and enjoy the eternal rewards of being part of God's plan to reach unsaved people.

God never puts pressure in any way on people to give, as we see from the Scriptures.

> **2 Corinthians 9:6-7:**
> **"But this I say: He who sows sparingly will also reap sparingly, and he who sows bountifully will also reap bountifully. So let each one give as he purposes in his heart, not grudgingly or of necessity; for God loves a cheerful giver."**

In 2 Corinthians chapters 8 and 9, the apostle Paul is teaching the subject of financial prosperity. He speaks of how Jesus was rich and then became poor so that through His poverty we might become rich. Paul speaks of this as grace.

Grace is God's willingness to use His power on our behalf even though we don't deserve it. Then the apostle under the inspiration of the Holy Spirit connects the meeting of our needs to giving. He calls this kind of giving sowing seeds and tells us that God provides us with seeds to sow and the bread to eat all in the exercise of His grace toward us because of Jesus Christ. Paul does not mention the tithe directly here but the principles he teaches govern all areas of giving including tithing.

Then in 2 Corinthians 9:6-7 Paul teaches us not to give sparingly but to give bountifully. He teaches us that each one should give as he purposes in his own heart, not grudgingly or of necessity because God loves a cheerful giver. The literal translation says, "not out of grief or necessity ..." God does not want any one of us to give with a heart full of grief. God is totally against grief. Jesus Christ at the cross bore the totality of our grief.

Isaiah 53:4:
"Surely He has borne our griefs
And carried our sorrows;
Yet we esteemed Him stricken,
Smitten by God, and afflicted."

Grief is an absolute red light and God will not have us live with grief or sorrow in our hearts. If you have to give tithes or offerings with grief or sorrow in your heart it would do you absolutely no good and I suggest you don't do it.

Grief means sadness, sorrow and heaviness of heart. The dictionary defines grief as deep and poignant distress caused by or as if by bereavement. In other words, grief is associated with a sense of loss. When you give tithes with an attitude that you are losing your money, that kind of giving will be accompanied with grief. That kind of tithing will not benefit you.

When we study this word even further it opens a can of worms. Looking at the Aramaic we find that the same word used for grief can also be translated as "to force, to compel, compulsion, reluctant, unwilling". The word means "something disagreeable and disgusting and loathsome".

It is naturally inbuilt within our nature as human beings that when we are being forced and compelled to do anything, it becomes disagreeable and loathsome to us. That is why there is no joy in religion and legalism because they make you do things against your will and desires. Bondage of any kind including religious bondage is as loathsome to the human nature as it is to God.

This is why the subject of tithing when approached from a legalistic angle breeds rebellion, disagreement, and reluctance among people. God never intended for us to give tithes and offerings in this way. God connected your tithing with the supernatural supply of your needs. It is something you should do with a joyful and willing heart. Truth by its very nature breeds freedom in all areas of life.

John 8:31:

"Then Jesus said to those Jews who believed Him, 'If you abide in My word, you are My disciples indeed. And you shall know the truth, and the truth shall make you free.'"

Someone referred to the tithe as a tax in the kingdom of God, but this cannot be true because taxes have the backing of the law and the law enforcement agencies behind them and if you fail to pay your taxes, law enforcement comes after you. The might of governments compels people to pay taxes and that is why to a very large extent people do it grudgingly and reluctantly. Tithing on the other hand, is something God wants you to do with a heart of understanding, willingly and joyfully because you know that it will come back to benefit you.

2 Corinthians 9:7 says we are to give "each one as he chose in his heart, not of grief or of necessity; for God loves a cheerful giver" (NASB Interlinear Translation).

This is a general principle which governs all areas of giving which includes tithing. The word "necessity" is the Greek word "anagkes" and it means "compelling force as opposed to willingness".

If you were walking down the street and someone came to you and put a gun to your head and said, "your money or your life" and you gave them your money, would you say you gave them your money willingly? No, that would be money you were compelled or forced to give. In the same way if a preacher told you: "If you don't tithe you are a God-robber and therefore you are going to hell," and in order to avoid going to hell you tithed. Do you call that giving your tithe willingly or by force? If you tithed that way, you would have done it under pressure. This is exactly what God is against as He instructs us in His word. This is why many have not reaped the benefits of tithing.

The Greek "anagkes" translated as "necessity", literally means "up-compress" which gives the sense of something being squeezed or forced out of you.

In other words, the apostle Paul under the inspiration of the Holy Spirit teaches us that we should not give (and that includes tithing) with the attitude and feeling that it is being squeezed or forced out of us. That is precisely what many preachers have done through religious and legalistic manipulation. When you give in response to this kind of religious and legalistic manipulation you are only enriching one person to your own detriment: that is the preacher who quotes God's word out of context to squeeze your money out of you. This is why the apostle Paul would not even receive an offering until he had taken the time to teach the people about finances, giving them an understanding of God's financial plan for their lives, and they gave willingly with joyful hearts and God blessed them through their giving.

2 Corinthians 9:7:

"So let each one give as he purposes in his heart, not grudgingly or of necessity; for God loves a cheerful giver."

That means each one should come to a firm decision and resolve before giving and that includes tithing. You can only do that with a heart of understanding. This is where many ministers have failed miserably. They have been very strong in collecting the tithes of the people but very weak in bringing them sound understanding along these lines.

If you are giving with a sense of anger, sadness, grief and heaviness in your heart and with the feeling that it is being squeezed and forced out of you against your will, I will advise that you put a hold on it for a moment and take the time to prayerfully study God's word until you come to the place where you are giving cheerfully, joyfully and in faith. Going to heaven and escaping hell is not based on tithing or giving money.

When we examine the words of God given through the prophet Malachi concerning tithing, we see a God who is not trying to pressure anyone into giving the tithe through guilt or condemnation but what we see is a God who is deeply interested in all aspects of our lives including our finances and who wants to intervene on our behalf and use His power to meet our needs. God wants to empower us financially and tithing is part of His financial plan for our lives.

21

LOVE'S APPEAL FOR PARTNERSHIP

Malachi 3:10:
"'Bring all the tithes into the storehouse,
That there may be food in My house,
And try Me now in this,'
Says the Lord of hosts,
'If I will not open for you the windows of heaven
And pour out for you such blessing
That there will not be room enough to receive it.'"

God instructs His people to bring all the tithes into the storehouse. He goes further by saying to them, "try Me now in this, if I will not open the windows of heaven and pour out a blessing ..."

In other words, He connects the tithe to the manifestation of the blessing in their lives.

The Hebrew word for "blessing" has to do with enlargement, increase and freedom in all areas of life including finances. The Lord connects the blessing of financial increase with the tithes of the people.

Then God uses a peculiar word here that makes us realise that He is not placing pressure of any kind on us in calling us to give the tithe.

It says, "and try Me now in this."

The Hebrew word translated as "now" is the word "na". Unfortunately, in translating this word as "now" we miss out on much of what God is saying here in this verse. In fact, the word "now" actually puts pressure on you, which would be contradictory to God's instructions to us in 2 Corinthians 9:6-7.

The Hebrew word "na" is a Hebrew particle of entreaty and exhortation. Many times, it is translated as "please" in the Old Testament.

The Hebrew-English interlinear ESV Old Testament puts it this way:

"... bring whole of the tithe into house of the store house that he may be food in house of me and test me PLEASE in this ..."

This is a word-for-word translation but take note of the word "please" in this translation.

God was using the word "please" because in the use of this word He takes the pressure off from the people. "Please" is not the language of law.

We use the word "please" in our daily language to convey kindness and politeness. When you say to someone "please give me a glass of water," you are not placing them under any kind of pressure whatsoever. It is an appeal on your part to them and you are saying to them to do it at their pleasure, volition, and choice.

1 John 4:16 tells us that God is Love and Malachi 3:6-12 is Love's appeal to His people.

It is a revelation of Love's intense desire to step in and be involved in our finances. It is Love's encouragement to us. The whole purpose of encouragement is to overcome reluctance, doublemindedness, hesitation, and fear.

When a baby is trying to walk, the parents are there all the time to encourage them. They don't get angry with the baby, threaten, curse, and condemn them for stumbling and falling while trying to walk. When the baby stands and tries to walk and then falls the parents encourage them, knowing that it is in trying and falling and stumbling that they eventually will perfect the act of walking. It is the same here. The Hebrew word "na" is a language of encouragement. That means you may fall and fail a few times as you start your tithing journey. You may not even be able to give your full tithe now because of the pressure of your financial situation but

God encourages you to take those baby steps and to keep trusting Him where you are and giving what you can until you are on your feet financially and able to bring the full tithe.

1 John 4:17-18:

"Love has been perfected among us in this: that we may have boldness in the day of judgment; because as He is, so are we in this world. There is no fear in love; but perfect love casts out fear, because fear involves torment. But he who fears has not been made perfect in love."

There is no fear in love because God is Love. God tells us why He does not want us operating in fear. That is because fear has torment in it.

God wants us to live free from the tormenting fear of lack, want and poverty. He also does not want us to bring our tithes and offering to Him out of tormenting fear that we would go to hell if we don't tithe or that He is angry with us for not tithing.

The instruction to tithe is not because God wants to burden you with other people's needs and problems but because He loves you and wants to be involved in all areas of your life including your finances.

1 Peter 5:6-7:

"Therefore humble yourselves under the mighty hand of God, that He may exalt you in due time, casting all your care upon Him, for He cares for you."

The NASB Interlinear Greek translation says: "... to Him it matters concerning you".

In other words, if it concerns you then it matters to God. He does not downplay any aspect of our lives. Everything about you matters to God including your finances and certainly He does not intend tithing to be a source of anxiety, pressure and worry to you.

22

THE HELPING HANDS OF TITHERS

The Hebrew word for "hand" also means to share, portion, part with or partnership. To have partnership in the gospel ministry of Jesus Christ means your hands are involved in getting it done.

It is this concept and principle of partnership that the apostle Paul communicates to the churches.

Philippians 1:3-6
"I thank my God upon every remembrance of you, always in every prayer of mine making request for you all with joy, for your fellowship in the gospel from the first day until now, being confident of this very thing, that He who has begun a good work in you will complete it until the day of Jesus Christ."

Notice the words "your fellowship in the gospel". This Greek word here literally means "partnership". Paul refers to the Philippian church as his partners in the gospel. They were giving him their helping hands in getting the gospel out to the world.

Paul does not mention the tithe directly, but the principle covers tithing. He saw the Philippian church as his partners, his covenant friends in delivering the gospel message to the nations of the world and this means they would also share in Paul's eternal rewards for fulfilling God's assignment. What an awesome privilege.

Here is the interesting thing: the Hebrew word for "friend" is a covenant word and it means " … two hands clasped together". The clasping of hands is a symbol of partnership, and we can in this sense call it covenant partnership. The act of tithing is an act of covenant partnership to get kingdom work done in the earth realm.

God calls us to clasp hands with Him through our tithing to get His kingdom work done in the earth realm and in that process His supernatural hand is united with our natural hands in our financial affairs. God is able with His mighty hands to hold us firmly in His grip and take us through whatever we may face in our financial affairs.

Acts 20:32-35:

"So now, brethren, I commend you to God and to the word of His grace, which is able to build you up and give you an inheritance among all those who are sanctified. I have coveted no one's silver or gold or apparel. Yes, you yourselves know that these hands have provided for my necessities, and for those who were with me. I have shown you in every way, by laboring like this, that you must support the weak. And remember the words of the Lord Jesus, that He said, 'It is more blessed to give than to receive.' "

The apostle Paul said: "I have shown in every way, by laboring like this, you must support the weak." He did not say " I have shown that by labouring like this you meet all your own needs in your own power." He placed supporting the weak in the first place before his own needs and that is how it should be with us.

The Greek word translated as "support" here means "to help". The Greek word is "anti-lambano" and it means "to get instead" or "in the place of". In other words, you are doing it in the place of somebody else who for some reason is unable to do it.

He said this is the example he set before them, so that by labouring they could support the weak. The Greek word for weak here means "to be without strength".

Paul stretched out his hands before the Ephesians and said: "You all know that THESE hands have served my needs and the needs of those with me." And that was the example he showed them, that by labouring with their own hands they would support "those without strength".

This Greek word "anti-lambano"' used in Acts 20:35 is translated into "helpers" in 1 Corinthians 12:28:

"And God has appointed these in the church: first apostles, second prophets, third teachers, after that miracles, then gifts of healings, helps, administrations, varieties of tongues."

We have the word "helpers" which means to " get instead of". In other words, by reason of your assignment you are unable to get certain things done and yet those things are crucial and vital to the accomplishment of your assignment.

The picture that comes to my mind is when as a medical doctor I am in theatre doing a caesarean section. There are several other people present in the theatre to do other things crucial to getting that caesarean section done. You have the anaesthetist, then you have the scrub nurse and then you have the runner nurse all there to do things in my place as the surgeon. When I need a particular type of suture material, I don't stop what I am doing for a moment to go get myself the sutures that I need. There is someone there to get it done instead of me. That is the concept involved in this Greek word translated as "helpers" or "support".

This is the principle of division of labour, which brings about effectiveness and efficiency by maximizing the use of available resources.

Then let us look at the Hebrew word for "tithe" in this connection, which is "aser".

This word is related to the word "helper" used in Genesis 2:18:

"And the Lord God said, 'It is not good that man should be alone; I will make him a helper comparable to him.'"

The Hebrew word translated as helper here is "ezer", which is related to the Hebrew word for tithe "aser". This word "ezer" means help in a manner that reduces another's responsibilities.

A helper relieves his partner of part of his obligation, enabling him to concentrate his energies in a more limited sphere so that he can fulfil the remaining part of his obligation more effectively.

The tither therefore helps those whom God has called into the ministry to focus their energies and time to the accomplishment of their God-given assignment and in that way, they are much more effective and efficient.

Paul said to the Ephesians believers: "This is the example or model that I have set before you all." The concept and principle of tithing is involved in this model.

GETTING PROMPT HELP TO THOSE WHO NEED IT

Acts 8:29-31:
"Then the Spirit said to Philip, 'Go near and overtake this chariot.'
So, Philip ran to him, and heard him reading the prophet Isaiah, and said, 'Do you understand what you are reading?'
And he said, 'How can I, unless someone guides me?' And he asked Philip to come up and sit with him."

The Ethiopian Eunuch had his Bible which contains God's provision of salvation for mankind. He was unable to understand it, however, and so could not get a hold of the provision of salvation. He needed help and God sent Philip down there to help. He was an evangelist by calling. He needed to be prepared for the assignment and stay ready to go wherever God was calling him.

That is where the helping hands of tithers are needed. It is by the helping hands of tithers that things like these get done promptly. The helping hands of tithers is what God uses to get help promptly to people like the Ethiopian Eunuch and help them get saved. There are those God calls to support the gospel with their finances through tithing and other forms of giving and there are those like Philip whom God calls to stay ready to go wherever he wants them to be and to be there as quickly as possible to deliver prompt help to those who need it.

Therefore, the principle of the tithe cuts right across Scriptures from the old to the entire new covenant.

The Ephesian church had not yet learned this principle and so Paul had to model it to them by taking time out of his busy ministry schedule to work and then using his earnings as seeds of blessing which went further than the financial limitations he was facing. He went beyond the financial limitations on him as he converted his earnings into seeds which he sowed into the gospel.

OPEN UP SUPERNATURAL SUPPLY

Ephesians 4:28:
"Let him who stole steal no longer, but rather let him labor, working with his hands what is good, that he may have something to give him who has need."

We see the words "hands" being used here again. God uses the hands of people.

When it comes to your finances God wants to use His supernatural ability to meet your needs, but your hands must be put to work. Your hands signify your talents, skills and abilities.

Even though it is not directly mentioned here, the principle of the tithe is implied here.

It says: "Work with your hands that you may have something to give." The Greek word translated as "give" means "to share". It is to give a portion of what you have.

Hence Ephesians 4:28 may be read this way: "... that he may have something to share with someone in need." In need of what? In need of a helping hand. By labouring in this way, your hands become helping hands. This is partnership at work.

Through working a man like this can get into partnership with his local church through tithing and other forms of giving to get the gospel out to those who need it. Together with others he is getting the gospel out to those who need it and at the same time his own needs are being met by God supernaturally.

When we look up this verse in the Aramaic translation, we get even more insight into what the Holy Spirit is communicating to us about the power of the gospel partnership of giving. The Aramaic word for "giving" here leads us to the cognate meaning "to open up".

Paul is teaching us how to open channels of God's supernatural supply through the partnership of giving which includes tithing.

This same principle is communicated to us in Malachi 3:10:

> "'**Bring all the tithes into the storehouse,**
> **That there may be food in My house,**
> **And try Me now in this,**'
> **Says the Lord of hosts,**
> '**If I will not open for you the windows of heaven**
> **And pour out for you such blessing**
> **That there will not be room enough to receive it.'"**

God is teaching us how to open up Heavens's supernatural supply for our benefit in this world and tithing is involved in it. God did not give us the principle of tithing to burden us and reduce us financially. He gave us this principle so that our finances can be multiplied supernaturally and so that His kingdom can go further and further in this world and reach more and more people and we can have the eternal rewards that come with it.

23

TITHE AND WEALTH CREATION

Tithing is not a practice limited to Israel which found its way to Christianity. In fact, tithing as a practice has been present in many cultures and religions from ancient times.

The Romans, Greeks, Carthaginians, Cretans Sicilians, Phoenicians, Chinese, Babylonians, Akkadians, Egyptians, Assyrians, Persians, Moroccans and South Arabians had tithing in one form or other in their cultural and religious practices.

According to Hebrews 7:4 Abraham gave Melchizedek the priest a tenth of the war spoils from the battle with Chedolaomer and his allies.

The Greeks, for example, had a similar practice after victory in warfare of gathering the spoils of war in heaps and then separating the top or best for their gods who they believed made them victorious in battle.

This has led many to believe and put forward the idea that tithing was imported by God from the cultures of the nations that surrounded Israel and assimilated it into her worship of the one true God. If this were the case, then it would undermine the notion of an all-wise and self-sufficient God.

> **Isaiah 40:13-14:**
> "Who has directed the Spirit of the Lord,
> Or as His counselor has taught Him?
> With whom did He take counsel, and who instructed Him,
> And taught Him in the path of justice?
> Who taught Him knowledge,
> And showed Him the way of understanding?"

No, God did not need to take counsel or draw knowledge from surrounding cultures or religions in instructing His covenant people in the way of Life.

> **Proverbs 6:23-24:**
> **"For the commandment is a lamp,**
> **And the law a light;**
> **Reproofs of instruction are the way of life,**
> **To keep you from the evil woman,**
> **From the flattering tongue of a seductress."**

God did not take anything from the religious cultures around Israel and incorporate it into His worship, rather Israel was chosen by God to be a light of the nations of the world.

> **Isaiah 49:6:**
> **"Indeed He says,**
> **'It is too small a thing that You should be My Servant**
> **To raise up the tribes of Jacob,**
> **And to restore the preserved ones of Israel;**
> **I will also give You as a light to the Gentiles,**
> **That You should be My salvation to the ends of the earth.'"**

It is wrong to assume that God borrowed practices from other religions into His worship as if He was deficient in understanding, knowledge and wisdom. On the contrary the reverse is what must have happened. The tithe came forth to humanity in ancient times as divine revelation of the worship of the one true God of the universe and as a principle of prosperity. It was so successful in the creation of wealth that as human beings abandoned the worship of the one true God and walked more and more in darkness, they non-the-less took this practice of tithing with them into their religious and cultural practices. That, however, does not invalidate it as a genuine principle of God.

Genesis is the book of beginnings and the beginnings of anything within the human family can be traced in this book.

The first mention of the tithe in Genesis therefore gives us insight when the revelation of it came into the human family. It is mentioned in connection with two cardinal characters in the Bible. One of them is Melchizedek and the other is Abraham.

God called Abraham from Ur of the Chaldees as the world was beginning to slide deeper and deeper into the darkness of idolatry following Noah's flood and the confusion of languages at the Tower of Babel.

God was getting ready to make a fresh start with the human race through Abraham that would culminate in Jesus dying at the cross thereby making available salvation as we know it and resulting in the millennial reign of Jesus Christ and beyond.

Melchizedek on the other hand is the strange Bible figure that links the era before and after the flood of Noah with the call of Abraham right into the modern era.

In Melchizedek, is embodied the revelation and instructions of God to the human family from the days of Adam right to that encounter with Abraham in Genesis 14 where tithing is first mentioned.

Yes, it is true that in the book of Genesis, Melchizedek who was king of the city called Salem, which turns out to be a modern Jerusalem, is a mysterious figure.

The mystery and silence about his person however are deliberate and inspired on the part of the Holy Spirit to simulate the coming priesthood of Jesus Christ as the basis of all that God was about to do with Abraham and the nation of Israel and by extension the human family. Hence the Bible says he, Melchizedek, was "without father, without mother, without genealogy, having neither beginning of days nor end of life" that is according to the inspired records of the Bible.

However, reliable extrabiblical sources give us information as to who this Bible figure called Melchizedek in fact was. The ancient book of Jasher, which is regarded as a reliable historical source and is mentioned in the Bible, identifies Melchizedek as Shem the son of Noah.

In this event it refers to him with the title Adonizedek, which was also the title of subsequent kings of Jerusalem.

The Stone edition of the Tanach (Old Testament) commenting on Genesis 14:18 says the following: "... after meeting Abraham at the valley of shaveh, the king of Sodom escorted him to the city of Salem (= Jerusalem) where they were met by Melchizedek, whom the sages identify as Shem, the son of Noah."

If it is true, that this mysterious Bible Character called Melchizedek was in fact Shem then it gives us a lot of insight into the practice of tithing as a divine revelation in connection with the worship of God. A principle of which transcends generations until our time today.

Shem remained true to the worship of the one true God and creator of the universe and stayed with the revelation of God as he received it not only from his father, Noah, but from those who knew God and worshipped Him before the flood. He embodied all that revelation, understanding and wisdom in his time. Through him therefore as priest of the most high God, the knowledge and practice of tithing must have been transmitted to his generation and beyond. As we know, Shem lived to a great old age after the flood.

The seder Olam, which is a reliable chronological account book from creation to the time of the second temple, says the following concerning Methuselah, Shem, and Jacob.

"Methuselah learned directly from Adam since he was born 243 years before Adam's death. Shem learned directly from Methuselah since he was born 98 years before Methuselah's death. Jacob learned directly from Shem since he was born 50 years before Shem's death. Jacob's birth was also 16 years before Abraham's death. These four men lived through 22 generations".

In the light of all the above, we can see the meeting of Abraham and Melchizedek was a landmark event. It is as if the generation that survived the flood with the repository of its knowledge of God and the worship of God through Melchizedek passes the baton to generations that would come after including modern generations represented by Abraham.

The tithe is obviously part of that ancient repository of the knowledge of God passed down to us from the ancients. Indeed, it could be referred to as one of the ancient landmarks which we are not to remove (Proverbs 23:10).

Tithing as a principle of divine worship must have been so successful in the creation of wealth it was assimilated in the other cultures and idolatrous practices over time.

One evidence for this is in the Hebrew word for tithe which is the word "aser". This word is spelt ayin-sin-reish in the Hebrew language. However, the Hebrew word "to enrich" and "rich" was not different in ancient times. It is the word "asher" which is spelt "ayin-shin-reish". In the word "tithe", we have the Hebrew letter "sin" whereas in the Hebrew word for "rich" or "enrich", we have the Hebrew letter "shin". However, to the ancients these two letters where one and the same. In the minds of the ancients there was no separation between the practice of tithing and the building of wealth. Faithfulness in tithing has always been involved in the building of wealth especially generational wealth from a Biblical standpoint.

One example of building of generational wealth on the principle of tithing is the example of Mr. Alexander Kerr who started the Kerr Glass manufacturing company in the USA.

He had earlier in 1902 made a vow to God to set aside ten percent of his income for the work of the Lord and within three months of that that vow, the unexpected happened and he was able with practically all the money he had to start Kerr Glass manufacturing company which later became one of America's largest glass manufacturing companies.

At the time of the San Francisco earthquakes, wildfires started that seemed to engulf the site of his business. People thought that would be the end of him and his business as the wildfires would certainly ravage everything within the premises of his glass factory. The factory itself was a two-story wooden building and within the premises were huge tanks where the glass was kept melted at a very high temperature, which itself was fuel for the raging fires.

Mr. Kerr's faith in his God and the tithing covenant never wavered as he believed God would honour His promises and the devourer would be kept out of his property.

God came through for him and the premises of his business was supernaturally spared. It was widely acknowledged at that time as nothing short of a miracle of God.

Mr. Kerr went on to be a successful and wealthy businessman, as he tithed every business in which he was involved. He left behind a rich heritage for generations after him. Until his death in 1912 he continued to espouse the blessings and riches that come with tithing.

24

STEPS TO SUCCESSFUL TITHING

Isaiah 48:17:
"Thus says the Lord, your Redeemer,
The Holy One of Israel:
'I am the Lord your God,
Who teaches you to profit,
Who leads you by the way you should go.'"

Obedience to God's instructions ultimately leads to increase in all areas of life.

God's instructions in the Bible regarding tithing are there for our good and not to ruin us financially.

The Scripture above says: "God teaches or instructs us to profit …"

The Hebrew word translated as "profit" is "yaal" which means to benefit, to be valuable, to progress and to flourish. The same word means "to be effective and efficient". This "profit" is not limited to some aspects of our lives and to the neglect of others.

God's instructions to us including in the area of tithings is to benefit us, cause us to be more valuable, to progress, flourish and to become effective and efficient.

When you are effective you get the right things done and when you are efficient you cut out waste and get more done with less. This certainly has been the testimonies of tithers down through the years. When people tithed in line with instructions in the Bible, they have certainly been able to get more done with what is left than they would have had they kept it all to themselves.

Notice also it says: " ... His instructions make us more valuable", and the marketplace always delivers monetary rewards for value.

God said when we bring in our tithes He will "open the windows of heaven and pour out a blessing ..." This does not mean a rain of dollars or silver and gold from heaven, but one way God makes that happen is by giving us ideas that solve problems for which people are looking for answers. That will certainly create value in the marketplace, which brings about financial rewards that brings about the creation of wealth.

One area of difficulty and controversy among believers today is where to take their tithes since there are no clear-cut instructions in the New Testament about this. However, by studying God's instructions to the nation of Israel on tithing we can get insight to guide us.

Deuteronomy 26:1-2:

"And it shall be, when you come into the land which the Lord your God is giving you as an inheritance, and you possess it and dwell in it, that you shall take some of the first of all the produce of the ground, which you shall bring from your land that the Lord your God is giving you, and put it in a basket and go to the place where the Lord your God chooses to make His name abide."

Deuteronomy 26 is Israel's national confession which applied to two institutions as they came into their God-given land.

It applied to the offering of the first fruits of selected agricultural products of the land and the tithe.

In Deuteronomy chapter 26 God gave Israel specific instructions of the geographical location they were to take their tithes to. We don't see any such instructions in the New Testament. This is one area where we can say the practice of tithing under the old covenant is different from what obtains in the New Testament, but the principles are the same.

In the Old Testament worship was centralised to where the temple and the priesthood were located and so God told them specifically to take their tithes to that particular location. In the new Covenant worship is not localised to a building or a physical location.

> ### John 4:23-24:
> **"But the hour is coming, and now is, when the true worshipers will worship the Father in spirit and truth; for the Father is seeking such to worship Him. God is Spirit, and those who worship Him must worship in spirit and truth."**

Worship in the New Testament is in the spirit because when we get born again our spirits become the dwelling place of the Holy Spirit and that is where we contact God and that is where our worship flows from.

> ### Philippians 3:3:
> **"For we are the circumcision, who worship God in the Spirit, rejoice in Christ Jesus, and have no confidence in the flesh."**

In the New Testament the reborn spirit is where we contact God through the instrument of His word. This is one reason why we don't find specific instructions on where to take our tithes as we have in the Old Testament.

In the Old Testament Israel took their tithes to the temple which is where the priests carried out their duties but in the New Testament the believer is the temple of the Living God.

> ### 1 Corinthians 3:16:
> **"Do you not know that you are the temple of God and that the Spirit of God dwells in you?"**

If you are born again then you as a spirit being are the temple of the Living God. That is where you contact God through His word and not in a physical building as Israel did under the old covenant.

There is a place for the gathering of Christians for fellowship as the word of God instructs us to do, but the physical building where we gather for our fellowship meetings is not the temple of God.

Hebrews 10:25:

" ... not forsaking the assembling of ourselves together, as is the manner of some, but exhorting one another, and so much the more as you see the Day approaching."

Believers individually and collectively are the temple of God. However, we need the fellowship of other believers and God's word instructs us to be part of the fellowship of believers or what can be referred to as local church assemblies.

1 John 1:7:

"But if we walk in the light as He is in the light, we have fellowship with one another, and the blood of Jesus Christ His Son cleanses us from all sin."

This is therefore one fundamental area where the practice of tithing must be different from the Old Testament to the New Testament because Israel had a physical temple under the Old Testament but we in the New Testament do not have one. The principle of the tithe however remains the same throughout.

Let's look at some aspects of the instructions God gave Israel in Deuteronomy 26 that can guide us in the New Testament.

1. YOU SHALL TAKE

The first thing God told Israel when it comes to the tithing was: " ... you shall take".

The idea here is that this is an action initiated within you and not under any form of compulsion or force. It is like breathing. When you are in a normal healthy state of life you are not aware of your breathing. The moment you become aware of your breathing, and you are struggling to breath, and you are questioning your own breathing, something is already wrong with your health, and you need the doctor to step in and fix it.

The Bible says God loves a cheerful giver and that applies to your tithing. If it is not bringing you joy and you have the sense that it is being squeezed out of you then that is a red signal and you need to stop, get your Bible out and study God's word prayerfully on how to proceed from where you are.

The next thing we see in this instruction is in the word "take" itself.

The Hebrew word is "leqach" and this word means " take for yourself". In other words, " take for your own good and benefit."

Again, let us illustrate this from the point of view of your health. Let's say you are sick and went to consult with your physician and after he has listened to you and examined you, he came to a diagnosis and wrote a prescription for you. Then he hands the prescription to you, saying "take this". What did he mean by that? You took the prescription from him but who did you take it for? Of course, you were taking it for you own benefit, for your own recovery from illness. You would take that prescription to the pharmacy and pay some money for the medication, but the pharmacist is not the one who is the ultimate beneficiary of that prescription, you are.

This is the sense in which the word " take" is used in Deuteronomy 26 as God instructed the people to bring their tithes. It was for their good and benefit. God said to the people: "Take the tithe and go the temple where the priest is." But they were taking it for their good and benefit.

It is the same today. Tithing will bless you as it also goes forth to bring blessing to others. It is a win-win kingdom transaction.

2. YOU SHALL GO

The next instruction God gave Israel was that they were to go physically by themselves and hand in their tithes.

Again, in the New Testament this practice may not apply completely for several reasons. One reason today is that our tithes are in the form of money and money can be moved around today without any physical movement of the ones making the transfers.

We can however learn from this instruction that God gave Israel. What does the New Testament say about our feet and walking today?

2 Corinthians 5:7:
"For we walk by faith, not by sight."

Walking brings in the element of faith into our tithing. If there is no element of faith in our tithing, then it will never please God.

If you are tithing just to fulfil some legal requirement or to escape going to hell or be a member in good standing in your church or to be seen to be a great tither like the Pharisees of the Old Testament, you are doing it with the wrong motives, and it is not pleasing God.

Hebrews 11:6:
"But without faith it is impossible to please Him, for he who comes to God must believe that He is, and that He is a rewarder of those who diligently seek Him."

When you tithe mix faith with your tithing, and it will be pleasing to God, and you will receive the rewards of tithing.

How does faith come? Romans 10:17 says: "So then faith comes by hearing and hearing by the word of God." Build a list of Scriptures that have to do with tithing and giving and the promises attached to them and be sure to recite these Scriptures to yourself continually as you remind God of what His promises are to you when you tithe.

Isaiah 43:26:
"Put Me in remembrance;
Let us contend together;
State your case, that you may be acquitted."
God wants us to bring His word back to Him in remembrance.

Putting God in remembrance does not mean He forgets His promises. It simply means if God is going to keep His covenant in your life you have something to do about it. You have to voice His word, His promises back to Him which creates faith on your part and when God's word comes back to Him in faith, He takes action to make it good on your behalf. Therefore, take time to give voice to God's tithing promises to you.

> **Deuteronomy 26:14-15:**
> "I have not eaten any of it when in mourning, nor have I removed any of it for an unclean use, nor given any of it for the dead. I have obeyed the voice of the Lord my God, and have done according to all that You have commanded me. Look down from Your holy habitation, from heaven, and bless Your people Israel and the land which You have given us, just as You swore to our fathers, 'a land flowing with milk and honey.'"

This is like saying: "Lord, I have done according to your word, I obeyed you, I ask you now to enforce your tithing promises in my life and circumstances."

3. HOPE SETS THE GOAL

God told the children: " ... you take the tithe and go ..."

We are looking at this word "go". First, we have seen that the element of faith is involved in it for the Bible says we walk by faith and not by sight. Tithing has to be done by faith. If you pay attention to natural financial circumstances and the condition of the economy, you will never give tithes.

> **Ecclesiastes 11.4**
> "He who observes the wind will not sow,
> And he who regards the clouds will not reap."

God told Israel to take their tithes and go with their own feet to the place of tithing which was the temple. The Hebrew word translated as "go" is "halach", which means not just walking but taking progressive steps of movement toward a goal or destination. That means when we give our tithes we should have before us a goal. What is the goal? It is the expected or predetermined outcome of your tithing. God has a goal for your tithing, an expected outcome.

Jeremiah 29:11:

"For I know the thoughts that I think toward you, says the Lord, thoughts of peace and not of evil, to give you a future and a hope."

The outcome or goal God has in mind for us is financial peace when we tithe. That is wholeness in our finances. God wants us to be where our financial needs are fully taken care of. When we give our tithes, we should have that goal in mind. That is our expectancy, and it is this hope or expectancy that creates the goal.

Hope is very important to faith because hope is what sets the goal for faith and where there is no hope faith has nothing to bring into manifestation. This is the reason why tithing has not worked for many. They have no hope when they tithe. They have no expectation of God. They are doing it to fulfil a legalistic and religious requirement. When you come to God with your tithes, come with hope in your heart. Come to God expecting Him to honour the tithing promises He has made to you in His word.

Hebrews 11:1:

"Now faith is the substance of things hoped for, the evidence of things not seen."

The twentieth century translation puts it this way:

"Faith is the realization of things hoped for ..."

Without hope faith has nothing to realize or bring into the realm of physical reality.

The New English Bible Translation of Hebrews 11:1:

"And what is Faith? Faith gives substance to our hopes."

Without hope which creates the goal, faith has nothing to give substance to.

Always come to God with an expectancy that is created within you from His promises when you give your tithes.

Learn to see all needs being met supernaturally when you tithe. Learn to see with the inner eye of faith the bills paid off through God's supernatural power and see all debts being cleared off through the inner eye of faith as you tithe. That is Bible hope setting the goal for faith.

4. THE LAW OF PROGRESSION

Many have become disillusioned in their faith life, their giving and tithing because they did it a few times and did not see immediate results and so they quit. But when we look into the instructions God gave to the nation of Israel concerning giving and tithing, we see built into these instructions the law of progression.

God told them: " ... you shall take and go ..."

Looking further into this Hebrew word translated as "go", which is the word "halach", we see the law of progression hidden within it.

This Hebrew word means not just to walk but it also means: " ... step by step progress toward a goal".

Hope sets the goal when we are operating in the principle of tithing. Our hope comes from the promises God has given us connected to giving and tithing.

God said the overall outcome He desires for all areas of our life including our finances, is peace.

The Hebrew word for peace means: " ... nothing broken and nothing missing".

When you are financially broke and you are unable to have your needs met, you are not in financial peace.

God wants to bring you out of that condition and tithing is part of His plan to get you there.

God wants you supernaturally and fully financed by His power. This is the goal and outcome God has in mind for you.

However, you will not necessarily get there with one step of your faith. It will take you a period of consistent actions in faith. This is the law of progression. You won't necessarily get there just because you put God's principles of tithing, giving, and believing into operation once or twice, three times or even four times. God wants us to be prepared for the long haul when walking by faith and never quit.

The law of progression means that success does not come from one giant move but a series of consistent actions over time. God has guaranteed us the outcome of financial wholeness when we stick with His word, but it is a process to get there and may take time that will test our ability to endure.

Implied in the Hebrew word translated as "go" (halach) is consistency of action with our eyes set and focussed on the guaranteed outcome in Christ Jesus.

The law of consistency means you will flounder sometimes, but you will get back on your feet, get your eyes back on the goal and keep going and getting better with each step you take.

The law of progression takes you through a process of character building that prepares you for the financial destination God has for you.

We can see the law of progression in the life of Isaac as God in covenant faithfulness blessed him financially.

Genesis 26:12-14:

"Then Isaac sowed in that land and reaped in the same year a hundredfold; and the Lord blessed him. The man began to prosper, and continued prospering until he became very prosperous; for he had possessions of flocks and possessions of herds and a great number of servants. So, the Philistines envied him."

Everret Fox's translation of verse 13 says: " ... the man became great, and went on, went on becoming greater until he was exceedingly great."

He went on and went on. That is the law of progression at work. He started small but stayed with the principle and kept on going with it until he became exceedingly great.

Hebrews 10:35-36:

"Therefore, do not cast away your confidence, which has great reward. For you have need of endurance, so that after you have done the will of God, you may receive the promise."

There are promises, benefits and rewards attached to tithing and it is by patience we receive them. Remember the law of progression as you operate by the kingdom principle of tithing.

5. THE PRIEST OF THAT DAY

In Deuteronomy 26:3 God told Israel in this national tithing chapter:

> **"And you shall go to the one who is priest in those days, and say to him, 'I declare today to the Lord your God that I have come to the country which the Lord swore to our fathers to give us.'"**

The literal translation says: "… you shall go to the priest who IS in those days…"

We see again from this Scripture why most of the New Testament is silent on this subject of tithing and even why Jesus Christ Himself did not speak much on it.

The reason is that the Levitical Priesthood in the time of Jesus Christ was about to pass away, and it passed away when Jesus finally shed His blood as the final sacrifice of that old covenant.

Just ask yourself where in the new covenant is this New Priesthood of Jesus Christ mentioned explicitly? Nowhere else but in the book of Hebrews and that is where the subject of tithing is first mentioned in the New Testament.

God says to His people under the old covenant: " … go to the one who is priest in those days …"

That referred to the one who occupied the office of High Office. The one who is High Priest in our day is Jesus Christ.

> **Hebrews 8:1:**
> **"Now this is the main point of the things we are saying: We have such a High Priest, who is seated at the right hand of the throne of the Majesty in the heavens."**

Jesus Christ is the one to whom we bring our tithes in the New Testament.

There are pastors today who erroneously preach that the tithe belongs to them. Well, that is a form of robbery also, because the tithe belongs to Jesus Christ and not to one single person in the church.

They argue that when the Bible speaks about the priest it speaks about them. That again is wrong. Jesus Christ is the High Priest over us all but in the New Testament, God's word refers to us all as body of priests.

1 Peter 2:9:
"But you are a chosen generation, a royal priesthood, a holy nation, His own special people, that you may proclaim the praises of Him who called you out of darkness into His marvelous light."

The priesthood does not refer to the office of the apostle, prophet, evangelist or pastor but refers to the entire body of Jesus Christ, which is the church.

Revelation 1:4-6:
"John, to the seven churches which are in Asia:

Grace to you and peace from Him who is and who was and who is to come, and from the seven Spirits who are before His throne, and from Jesus Christ, the faithful witness, the firstborn from the dead, and the ruler over the kings of the earth.

To Him who loved us and washed us from our sins in His own blood and has made us kings and priests to His God and Father, to Him be glory and dominion forever and ever."

It says: "He loves us (every one of us), and made us (every one of us), kings and priests unto God."

Your tithe belongs to Jesus Christ, and it is to Him you are to take it first and foremost. This is the instruction that we have from the word of God.

To take your tithes to Jesus is an act of worship and communion first and foremost and you ought to do it all the time.

6. I DECLARE

The people were to make their confession before the High Priest. They were to say: " I declare this day to the Lord your God that I have come to the country which the Lord swore to our fathers to give us."

It was a confession of God's faithfulness manifesting in their ability to tithe.

> **Hebrews 3:1:**
> **"Therefore, holy brethren, partakers of the heavenly calling, consider the Apostle and High Priest of our confession, Christ Jesus."**

Jesus Christ is the High Priest of our confession and we come to Him with our tithes and make our confession of His faithfulness. It is His grace that makes us able to tithe.

> **Colossians 1:12-13:**
> **" … giving thanks to the Father who has qualified us to be partakers of the inheritance of the saints in the light. He has delivered us from the power of darkness and conveyed us into the kingdom of the Son of His love."**

The land of Israel is a type of the new birth where we are delivered from the kingdom of Darkness and are transferred into the kingdom of the Son of God's love, Jesus Christ. We can make that confession before our High Priest Jesus Christ with grateful hearts.

God brings in the law of confession into tithing. Faith works with confession. Fear works with confession. The two are opposites of the same coin. Poverty is activated and kept active by confessions of fear. Fear says: " The bills will never get paid and we are going down financially". Faith says: "I am willing and I am obedient, I will eat the good of the land and my God shall supply all my needs according to His riches in glory by Christ Jesus."

Faith is a spiritual law and confessions of lips are involved in putting that law to work.

The power of God is governed by spiritual law and to put that power to work in your life and for your good, you have to learn to cooperate with spiritual law.

Electrical power makes the wonders and pleasures of modern day living possible but to put that power to work safely for your benefit, you must learn to cooperate with the law of electricity. If you get out of line with the laws of electricity, that power can bring about great harm.

Proverbs 10:21:
"The lips of the righteous feed many,
But fools die for lack of wisdom.
The blessing of the Lord makes one rich,
And He adds no sorrow with it."

The words that you speak have everything to do with your financial prosperity. There is no point in bringing to Jesus Christ the High Priest your tithes and then denying Him the use of your words to turn your circumstances around. He works with your words to bless you on the earth.

Hosea 14:2:
"Take words with you,
And return to the Lord.
Say to Him,
'Take away all iniquity;
Receive us graciously,
For we will offer the sacrifices of our lips.'"

Through the shed blood of Jesus Christ, He has taken away all our iniqiuities and now we can offer to Him the sacrifice of lips: our words. He can work through our words now to enforce the covenant on the earth realm.

The verse above says "we offer the sacrifices of our lips". The more literal translation says "we will offer the calves of our lips".

Many are trapped in the negative circumstances and financial lack and are wondering why God does not help them. It is because they offer nothing to God with which to work in their situations. God works with our words to intervene in our lives and circumstances.

When we continually speak words that contradict and nullify God's word in our lives and circumstances we cannot expect God to be active in our lives.

The Hebrew word to "bear fruit" is related to this word translated as "calves". God's word bears fruit upon our lips.

Proverbs 18:21:
"Death and life are in the power of the tongue and those who love it will eat the fruit thereof."

The word of God says: " ... if you are willing and obedient you will eat the good of the land" (Is 1:19).

Your words can work to make you eat the best of the land. Your words can work to prosper you. That is the power of words. Not only will your words work to prosper you financially, your words will work to make you physically healthy.

No wonder the devil fights so much to keep this part of our lives under his control because that is the way he can keep God out of our lives and stay active.

Cows, bullocks, calves were the machinery of work and production in those days. Our words are the machinery by which God's provisions are delivered to us. "We offer to Him the calves of our lips."

The Hebrew word for "work" is "asah" and it means to take something and then shape it and form it into what you want or desire. It means to make, create and to form. That is creative power at work. The word of God has God's creative energy in it.

We can release God's creative power on earth through the spoken word and when we tithe, God wants us to release our faith using the power of words to cause the manifestation of the rewards of tithing to come forth.

God's creative power will cause a way to appear in our finances where there seems to be no way. Through the power of spoken words we are tapping unlimited power and putting it to work here on earth.

This is why God told Joshua: "My word shall not depart from your mouth", because that is where Satan seeks to turn off the power. Refuse to cooperate with Satan by not yielding your confession to him.

Hold fast to saying what God has declared about you and your finances in the face of all evidence to the contrary.

The Hebrew word translated as "declare" implies standing in the face of all appearances of opposition, contradiction and enemies and declaring your confession.

That is what faith does and God wants us to hold our tithes before our Great High Priest and make our confession of His faithfulness in the face of lack, want, unpaid bills and whatever else the enemy is coming against us with.

Like Paul we must say in the face of the contrary winds and storms of life: "Wherefore sirs be of good cheer for I believe God that it shall be as I have been told in the word of God" (Acts 27:25).

7. THE PRIEST SHALL TAKE

It says above: " … and the Priest shall take". The literal idea in this verse is that "the priest shall take it wholly to himself." In other words, from that moment it is in His possession wholly and completely.

That means once you take your tithes to Jesus Christ it is wholly and completely in His hands.

By extension also your entire finances are wholly and completely in His hands because the tithe represents the whole.

This means stop exercising any form of fear, worry, and anxiety about your financial situation. Look to Jesus Christ to see you through.

This also means from that moment you should look to Jesus Christ to direct you where to put your tithe because it is His.

Jesus Christ is the head and we, the church, are the body. We are in contact with Him and He can direct us.

Let Jesus Christ, the head of the church, direct you where to put your tithes. Jesus Christ as head of the church directs the financial operations of the church including how the tithes of His people are put to work on the earth today.

Colossians 1:18:
"And He is the head of the body, the church, who is the beginning, the firstborn from the dead, that in all things He may have the pre-eminence."

Notice it says Jesus Christ is the head of the body, which is the church, so that in all things which includes financial matters and matters of the tithe, Jesus Christ is to have pre-eminence.

It does not say the pastor, the bishop, the apostle, or evangelist is to have pre-eminence, but that Jesus Christ is to have pre-eminence.

The Literal translation says: "… that in all things Him, that is Jesus Christ is to HOLD FIRST PLACE."

If we all observed this principle in our personal lives and in the local churches there will be greater accountability, transparency in the way the finances of the church are put to work.

Handle your tithes prayerfully looking to Jesus Christ the Head of the church to guide you through His Holy Spirit and His word to where you should put it.

Romans 8:14:
"For as many as are led by the Spirit of God, these are sons of God."

The Lord will guide and direct you through His Holy Spirit in your spirit, but His guidance will be in line with His word and through His word.

Psalm 119:105:
"Your word is a lamp to my feet
And a light to my path."

By looking at the word of God we can see guidelines on where He wants our tithes to be taken to and how He wants our tithes to be put to work here on earth because our tithes do not go to heaven from where Jesus operates His priestly ministry. The tithes are received here on earth and put to work here on earth.

APPOINTED REPRESENTATIVES RECEIVE TITHES

Hebrews 7:8:
"Here mortal men receive tithes, but there he receives them, of whom it is witnessed that he lives."

The Levitical Priesthood of the old covenant has been wrapped up and laid aside since the sacrifice of Jesus Christ at the cross. God no longer recognises that order of priesthood for the collection of tithes on His behalf.

Hebrews 7:8 says, "Here mortal men receive tithes, but there he receives them ..."

These mortal men are those who receive tithes here on earth on behalf of Jesus Christ who is the High Priest of the new covenant.

He appoints them to act on His behalf on earth in receiving the tithes and putting it to work on earth here under His direction as Head of the church. This is a great responsibility that must be carried with great fear, trembling and integrity knowing that one day we shall all give an account before Him.

1 Corinthians 12:28:
"And God has appointed these in the church: first apostles, second prophets, third teachers, after that miracles, then gifts of healings, helps, administrations, varieties of tongues."

These are generally referred to as ministry gifts and they are at the forefront of the work of Jesus Christ in His priestly ministration today.

Ephesians 4:11-12 gives us the same list in a different format.

> **"And He Himself gave some to be apostles, some prophets, some evangelists, and some pastors and teachers, for the equipping of the saints for the work of ministry, for the edifying of the body of Christ."**

These are offices through which Jesus Christ as Head of the church ministers to the body and through the body ministers to the world.

Therefore, those whom He sets in these offices can act as His appointed representatives to receive the tithe and put it to work under His direction.

However, the local church should play a greater role, more than anything else in receiving the tithes of God's people and putting it to work under the direction of Jesus Christ the Head of the church. This is the model that we have in the book of Acts and this how Paul instructed churches.

> **1 Corinthians 16:1-2:**
> **"Now concerning the collection for the saints, as I have given orders to the churches of Galatia, so you must do also: On the first day of the week let each one of you lay something aside, storing up as he may prosper, that there be no collections when I come."**

He directs them to set aside as God prospers and that it should be taken to the local gathering of believers who would represent the local church and there give it.

25

THE GREATEST USE OF MONEY

Jesus Christ as our present day High Priest is the receiver of our tithes.

We have established that through the application of the law of first mention all the way from the book of Genesis.

Hebrews 3:1:
"Therefore, holy brethren, partakers of the heavenly calling, consider the Apostle and High Priest of our confession, Christ Jesus."

This Scripture tells us that we are partakers of His heavenly calling.

The word partaker means "partners or sharers with".

We are sharers with Jesus in His heavenly calling. What is this heavenly calling? The verse tells us "the Apostle and High Priest".

The literal meaning of the Greek word translated as "partner" is "with have". In other words, we are partners with Jesus. We have that calling with Him. He does not do it alone. He needs you and me to carry out His heavenly calling. What an awesome privilege we have in Christ Jesus!

Hebrews 8:1-2:
"Now this is the main point of the things we are saying: We have such a High Priest, who is seated at the right hand of the throne of the Majesty in the heavens, a Minister of the sanctuary and of the true tabernacle which the Lord erected, and not man."

We have an insight into the priestly ministry which He carries out from Heaven today.

The verse above says He is a minister of the sanctuary and of the true tabernacle. The Greek word translated as "sanctuary" literarily means "holy things".

As High Priest today Jesus Christ is a minister of holy things. Then we have the Greek word " minister", which is the word "leitourgos". This word in ordinary Greek language means "people work" or "people action".

Jesus' calling as High Priest today is doing "people work in holy things". He is working on behalf of people. He is working for us all today. He is preoccupied with our highest good. What a blessing! What rest that brings into our troubled spirits! Jesus works for people today to bring God's forgiveness, healing, deliverance and supernatural supply to them!

This is what ministry is all about. Ministry is about people and Jesus is the model and example of it.

The word "leitourgos" comes from two Greek words "leitos" which means "belonging to the public or people" and "ergon" which means "work". In other words, this means working for the people.

This word came to be used in religion to mean one who ministers in religious matters and in the translation of the Old Testament into Greek, the septuagint, the word was used in translating the Hebrew word "priest".

Yes! Jesus' Ministry today from the right hand of God is working for people everywhere. And we have that ministry with Him. We are partakers or partners with Him in His calling. What an awesome blessing and privilige has been granted us by the Heavenly Father.

Acts 10:38:

" ... how God anointed Jesus of Nazareth with the Holy Spirit and with power, who went about doing good and healing all who were oppressed by the devil, for God was with Him."

He went about in the power of the Holy Spirit doing good and healing all who were oppressed by the devil. That is people action. He is still doing it today as High Priest of the new covenant.

Hebrews 13:8:

"Jesus Christ is the same yesterday, today, and fore ver."

Jesus Christ in His present day ministry as lord High Priest is all about PEOPLE. He is doing everything He does today for people.

When we bring our tithes and offerings to Jesus Christ, He receives them from us and what does He do with them? He does not transfer all that money back into heaven. He does not need our money in heaven. He puts our tithes and offerings into "people work" here on earth.

Can you think of a greater use that your money can be put to on earth and can you think of a greater privilege than to be one of those Jesus appoints to be one of His representatives to collect His tithes and offerings and through you put it to people-action in this world with all the eternal rewards that come with it? But many are selfish and hard-hearted and in their selfishness and hard-heartedness abuse this privilege.

You put your tithes and offerings in the hands of Jesus Christ as partner with Him in His heavenly priestly calling. He in turn puts your money to work in reaching the lost with His gospel, in providing ministry to His people, in healing the sick and feeding the hungry and reaching the orphaned and the widowed, in visting prisoners and in doing mission work. Then He mulitplies it back to you and in the process meets your own needs supernaturally and in eternity you get to live with the rewards of this kind of giving.

There is nothing greater than this. There is no better or greater way to put your money to use in this world. This is the reason the devil fights it and will want us to spend our time arguing and fussing about it.

The time has come for us to move past all the argument and fussing and live as partners with Jesus Christ in this holy calling.

THE EXAMPLE OF PETER

Luke 5:1-3:

"So it was, as the multitude pressed about Him to hear the word of God, that He stood by the Lake of Gennesaret, and saw two boats standing by the lake; but the fishermen had gone from them and were washing their nets. Then He got into one of the boats, which was Simon's, and asked him to put out a little from the land. And He sat down and taught the multitudes from the boat."

Peter and his partners ran a fishing business. The Lake of Galilee was where they worked and made a living. On this particular night they worked themselves to exhaustion and took in nothing.

Jesus steps into the situation in the morning and shows them how to turn the situation around. He borrows their boat for a while and puts it into people-work or people-action.

The Bible says He sat in that boat and from there taught the people who were all hungry to receive His life-giving message.

When He had finished teaching them He turned to Peter and his friend to bless them with the returns of putting their boat to people-work.

Luke 5:4-7:

"When He had stopped speaking, He said to Simon, 'Launch out into the deep and let down your nets for a catch.'

"But Simon answered and said to Him, 'Master, we have toiled all night and caught nothing; nevertheless at Your word I will let down the net.' And when they had done this, they caught a great number of fish, and their net was breaking. So they signaled to their partners in the other boat to come and help them. And they came and filled both the boats, so that they began to sink."

Peter had toiled all night and from a natural perspective could not fathom how he could make a catch in that situation but decided to act on the words of Jesus Christ. The result was a haul of fish that was breaking the nets and sinking the boat. Together with his partners Peter could hardly take in the catch.

Through putting their boat into people-work with Jesus, Peter and his friends experienced a supernatural turn around of their situation.

Like Peter your situation may look gloomy and impossible to turn around. You may have bills and debts piling up with no way to go and no one to turn to but Jesus Christ who is the same yesterday, today, and forever.

Choose to go into partnership with Him today in His high priestly ministry of people-work.

Become a partner with Him in reaching people with His gospel of salvation and you will see Him manifest His power in your life and turn your circumstances around, plus in eternity you will live with rewards of being His partner in reaching people with His love and power here on earth.

Romans 12:2:
"And do not be conformed to this world, but be transformed by the renewing of your mind, that you may prove what is that good and acceptable and perfect will of God."

Transformation comes to our lives when we have our minds renewed by God's word and start seeing things God's way.

Begin the process of renewing your mind today to start seeing finances the kingdom way, the Jesus way and you will see your financial life transformed.

RECEIVE JESUS CHRIST AS LORD

Philippians 4:19:
"And my God shall supply all your need according to His riches in glory by Christ Jesus."

God wants all your needs to be met. He cares about everything that concerns you. The Bible says not even the sparrows are forgotten before God, and the hairs on your head are numbered.

Luke 12:6-7:
"Are not five sparrows sold for two copper coins? And not one of them is forgotten before God. But the very hairs of your head are all numbered. Do not fear therefore; you are of more value than many sparrows."

God cares about every detail of your life and wants to be part of your life and use His power to get your needs met. However, God's plan cannot become active in your life without Jesus Christ. It all begins when you make Jesus Christ Lord of your life. God's eternal salvation plan that covers all aspects of our lives in this world and reaches into eternity delivering us from eternal damnation is all based on the Lordship of Jesus Christ.

Hebrews 5:9-10:
"And having been perfected, He became the author of eternal salvation to all who obey Him, called by God as High Priest according to the order of Melchizedek."

Salvation means deliverance from sin and all its consequences and that includes eternal damnation. The consequences of sin include sickness and disease and poverty, but the salvation of Jesus Christ delivers us from all that. It all begins with making Jesus Christ Lord of your life.

Romans 10:8-10 tells us how God's salvation can be received by anybody:

> **"But what does it say? 'The word is near you, in your mouth and in your heart' (that is, the word of faith which we preach): that if you confess with your mouth the Lord Jesus and believe in your heart that God has raised Him from the dead, you will be saved. For with the heart one believes unto righteousness, and with the mouth confession is made unto salvation."**

It is a simple plan that involves believing in your heart and confessing His Lordship with your mouth. Receiving the salvation of Jesus Christ includes receiving God's total forgiveness for your sins and becoming a new creation in Christ Jesus. This enables you to begin a new life of salvation with God's total involvement as your Heavenly Father.

Now, pray the following prayer sincerely to receive total forgiveness, cleansing, and the new life available to you in Christ Jesus:

"Heavenly Father, I come to you just as I am in the name of your Son, Jesus Christ. The Bible says as many as come to you through His name, you will not cast out. You will receive them and give them eternal life in Christ.

"I repent of a life of sin. I believe Jesus took my sins on Himself, died in my place on the cross and received the punishment due to me. I believe You raised Him for my justification on the third day.

"Today, I confess and receive Jesus as my Lord and Saviour. I believe a new life is imparted to my spirit at this moment, I am born again by your Holy Spirit, and the blood of Jesus cleanses me from all sin.

"I will from this moment walk in the reality of my salvation in Christ Jesus.

In the mighty Name of Jesus, Amen."

If you just said the above prayer from your heart in faith, then Jesus Christ is now your Lord and Saviour, and you are a born-again child of the living God. This is the beginning of a new and exciting relationship between you, Jesus Christ and God the Father.

WELCOME TO THE FAMILY OF GOD!

Please contact me at abc@abettercovenant.org or visit the ministry website at www.abettercovenant.org for more teachings to help you grow and take full advantage of God's provision for you as His child.

Wherever you are, please join a local church where God's word, the Bible, is taught and preached and where you will have the support of a local network of fellow believers.

OTHER BOOKS BY DR. FELIX O. IDOLOR

Get Off the Treadmill and Live by Design.

Release the Power of God's Forgiveness in Your Life.

How to Receive the Provisions of the Covenant.

Nigeria Plan B? Christian Politics and Civil Government.

You can also subscribe to the ministry newsletter

Expect a Miracle Every Day with Jesus at www.abettercovenant.org

Or by sending your email address to abc@abettercovenant.org

REFERENCES

Bullinger, E.W. *How To Enjoy The Bible*. Republished by Kregel Inc, 1990, Grand Rapids Mi, USA, 1990.

Concordant Version Of The Old Testament, Concordant Publishing Concern, Almont Mi, USA, 2014.

Howard, George. *The Hebrew Gospel Of Matthew*, Mecer University Press, Macon Geogia USA, 1995.

Johnson, Ken. Th.d. *Ancient Seder Olam: A Christian Translation of the 2000-year-old scroll,* USA. 2006.

Marshall, Alfred. NASB Interlinear Greek-English New Testament, The Zondervan Cooperation, Grand Rapids Mi. USA, 1984.

Saphir, Adolph. *The Epistle To The Hebrews, Expository Lectures, 1875*, By Karen Ahvah Meshihit, Jerusalem, Republished 2003.

The Companion Bible, The Authorized Version of 1611, with notes and appendixes by E. W Bullinger. Kregel Publications,Grand Rapids, MI. USA, Republished 1999.

The Hebrew-English Interlinear Old Testament, Crossway, Wheaton Illinois 60187. USA, 2014.

The Pentateuch and Haftorahs, Hebrew Text English Translation & Commentaries, Soncino Press, London, 1960.

The Stone Edition Tanach, Mesorah Publications Ltd, New York,11232 USA, 2012.

Made in the USA
Middletown, DE
28 May 2024

54950190R00091